JAPA

117 Woodblock Prints

GYOKURANSAI SADAHIDE

Edited and with an Introduction by
CHARLES VILNIS

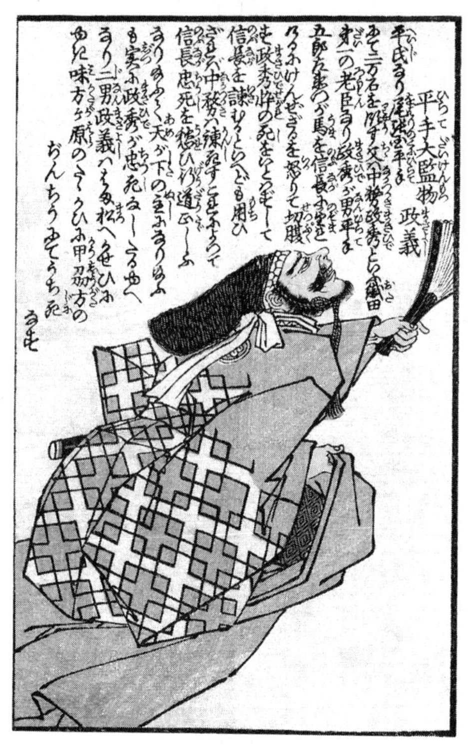

DOVER PUBLICATIONS, INC.
MINEOLA, NEW YORK

Copyright

Bibliographical Note

Japanese Warriors: 117 Woodblock Prints, first published by Dover Publications, Inc., in 2012, is a republication of a selection of plates from rare editions of *Eimei Hyakuyūden,* originally published in Japan in 1863. The physical condition of the original plates varies in quality; every attempt has been made to present them in the best possible manner. Plates 38 and 39, which have partial images, have been retained for the integrity of the selection.

Library of Congress Cataloging-in-Publication Data

Gyokuransai, Sadahide, 1807–1873.
Japanese warriors : 117 woodblock prints / edited and with an introduction by Charles Vilnis.
p. cm.
Japanese Warriors: 117 Woodblock Prints, first published by Dover Publications, Inc., in 2012, is a republication of a selection of plates from rare editions originally published in Japan in 1863.
ISBN-13: 978-0-486-48355-9
ISBN-10: 0-486-48355-X
1. Samurai in art. I. Vilnis, Charles. II. Gyokuransai Sadahide, 1807–1873. Works. Selections. III. Title.

NE1184.5.U83A4 2012
769.92—dc23

2012030155

Manufactured in the United States by Courier Corporation
48355X01
www.doverpublications.com

INTRODUCTION TO THE DOVER EDITION

CHARLES VILNIS

The collection *Eimei Hyakuyūden,* reproduced herein, is a worthy representative of the many volumes of *musha-e*—warrior prints—published in the late Tokugawa period. The warrior biographies of these "Tales of One Hundred Famous Warriors" were written by Chikazawa Kosan and the book published in the third year of the Bunkyū era [1863], a few years before the fall of the feudal regime based in Edo. Kosan was a known and respected historical scholar. To aid in its popularity, the publisher chose as illustrator Gyokuransai Sadahide, known not only for his warrior prints but also for his views of the new foreign trading center at Yokohama and for his bird's-eye views of city scenes. Sadahide [1807–73] was in the mainstream tradition of the Utagawa school of *ukiyo-e.* His teacher was Kunisada I, in turn the disciple of the great master Toyokuni I. Sadahide's work has always had an audience both in Japan and abroad. His draughtsmanship is skillful, his compositions dramatic and complex. He is a worthy representative of the late ukiyo-e printmakers of Japan at the end of the Tokugawa era and on into the new age of Emperor Meiji, after the fall of the old regime.

Always a beloved genre, Japanese warrior prints *(musha-e)* had become more popular than ever in the mid-nineteenth century, particularly as the old regime of the Tokugawa began to lose its grip on the country. The arrival of "strangers at the gates," as Western powers demanded entry; the approach of political transition as a consequence; and the impending danger of war ahead produced a nostalgia for an earlier heroic age of warriors.

Images of warriors had been a subject of art, visual and literary, before and throughout the Tokugawa era [1603–1868]. Historical and fictional figures from the long sweep of Japanese as well as Chinese history were the subject of such art. The violence that accompanied the end of the old Imperial rule during the thirteenth century had been immortalized in epics like the *Heike Monogatari* soon thereafter, and the heroes from that time become a part of the cultural canon. Chinese popular fiction from the Ming era (1368–1644), full of warriors, bandits, heroic men, and faithful women of every social class, was popular in Japan as well. Then there was the period of the "warring states" in Japan, which essentially occupied the whole of the sixteenth century. It was a war of all against all, as the disintegrating political culture spawned struggles for power between clan coalitions and produced three great dictators who tried to unite the warrior factions into an orderly system once again.

The last, Tokugawa Ieyasu, succeeded, and by a combination of overwhelming power and clever statecraft succeeded in keeping the clans and society as a whole under the authority of his family for 250 largely peaceful years. Yet, the stable era he created had its foundation in chaos and heroism, which later generations would look back on and immortalize. Strict cultural control over art and literature helped to maintain social order as the economy, the population, the wealth of the merchant class, and urbanization all proceeded. The inevitable unrest in a growing and changing Japan was suppressed, as was any artistic glorification of opposition to the status quo, the former by miltary power and the latter by a system of censorship. However, as the nineteenth century wore on and the future of the Tokugawa regime became unclear, the history of its creation in the midst of disorder became more topical, and the heroes of earlier, more dangerous, times became an increasingly popular subject for art.

The subjects of this book, the one hundred heroes, were all figures in the civil war waged during the Warring States period, stretching from 1467 to 1600. It began between rivals in and around the old capital of Kyōto, laying that city to waste and then spreading to the provinces. The period ended with the struggle of three successive unifiers to bring the competing clans under control. First, Oda Nobunaga; then, after his assassination,

Hideyoshi Toyotomi; and, finally, Tokugawa Ieyasu tried and eventually succeeded in imposing order and a new system of strict feudal governance. The de facto capital was moved far to the east, from the Imperial capital of Kyōto to Edo (modern day Tōkyō). A period of peace and relative prosperity and enormous population growth would follow, which made Edo the largest city in the world by the late seventeenth century and created a literate and cultured middle class in the three great cities of Edo, Ōsaka, and old Kyōto, with many urban centers elsewhere as well.

The story of those 130 years of civil war that transformed Japan was written in the *Eimei Hyakuyūden* as biography and expressed as dramatic popular art. There is little snobbery in the selection of the included historical figures. The heroes span the hierarchy from clan heads to empire builders. It might be fruitful to examine a few of the biographical notes on the warriors to see what the reader of this work would have discovered in 1863. The ordering is as arbitrary as in the original work—it simply follows randomly along from the beginning of volume one to the end of volume three, as the heroes appeared.

It is interesting that all of the biographies are roughly the same length, whether the subject was a long-forgotten and quite minor character or one of the unifiers, like Hideyoshi Toyotomi himself. The importance of the image in this picture book meant a uniformity of treatment. The artist and his images ruled the arrangement of the text; the historical captions were a vehicle for the dramatic artistry.

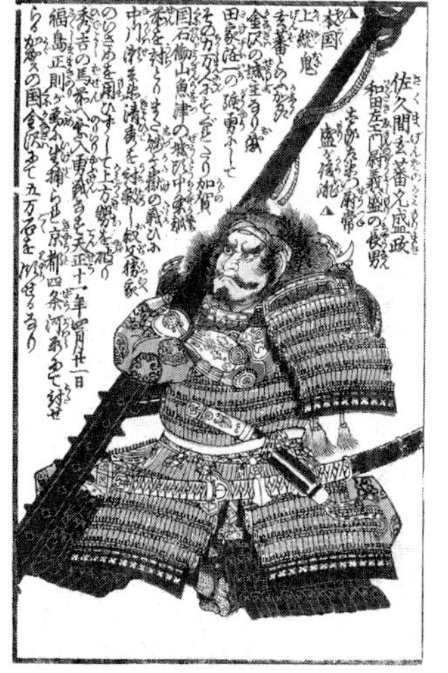

The figure on the verso of the 8th sheet in volume one [Plate 15] is Sakuma Gemba Morimasa [1554–1583], a retainer and general for the Shibata clan, vassals of the great

Oda Nobunaga, the first of the three unifiers who arose at the end of the civil wars. Known for his daring and aggression, he was nicknamed "onigemba," or "demon gemba." In the struggle against Hideyoshi Toyotomi, Oda's strongest rival, Sakuma disobeyed his leige lord while beseiging an enemy stronghold and did not retreat in the face of a superior army. His own troops routed and he was captured and subsequently beheaded when brought back to Kyoto, all before his thirtieth birthday.

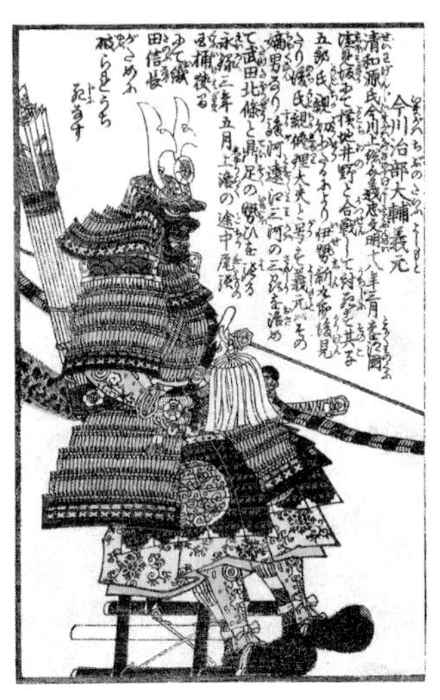

Imagawa Yoshimoto [1519–1560] occupies the verso of the 14th sheet in volume one [Plate 27]. Claiming relationship to the Imperial line from the ninth century and thus from the traditional aristocracy, the Imagawa clan was a powerful one with deep historical roots. As the second son, Yoshimoto was sent to a temple, but when his elder brother died he succeeded, through a family struggle, in assuming the clan headship. United to the family of the powerful lord Takeda Shingen through marriage, the Imagawas became increasingly influential as a result of Yoshimoto and Shingen's political sagacity and military genius. In a series of struggles with the rising Oda clan, Yoshimoto achieved great success, until overconfidence led him to a fatal error and his superior force was routed by a small contingent of Oda's allies, a defeat that saw him killed in battle. After that, the Imagawas gradually lost their primacy, and their land ultimately was seized by their erstwhile ally Takeda Shingen. The family was later protected by Tokugawa Ieyasu, the third and finally successful unifier who created the stable feudal polity centered on Edo.

Another vassal of Takeda Shingen, Kiso Yoshimasa [1540–1595], had his domain captured in battle by the Takeda but was brought into the clan via marriage. In volume two, on the verso of sheet 9 [Plate 57], Yoshimasa's story occupies the same amount of space as any other of the heroes, but his status as hero is a bit murky since he is primarily known as a traitor to his lord. Takeda Shingen died in 1573, and his son ruled in his stead, poorly. He alienated many of the Takeda vassals, including Yoshimasa, whose betrayal of the Takeda in 1582 contributed to their final and irrevocable defeat and total extermination by a combined force of the Oda, the Hojo, and the Tokugawa armies. Kiso survived but was deprived of his lands by the second great unifier, Hideyoshi Toyotomi, who succeeded Oda Nobunaga after his assassination.

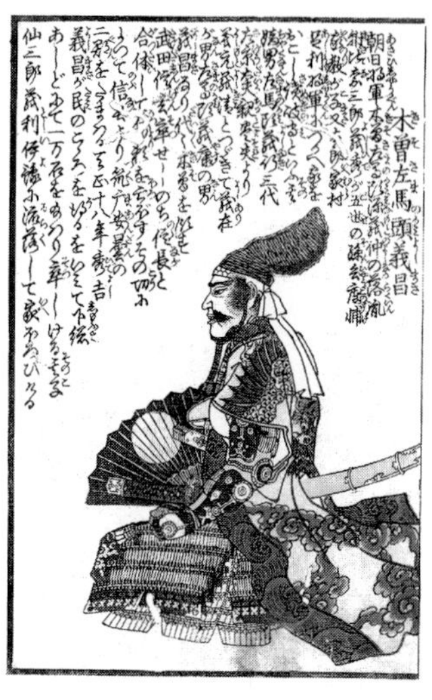

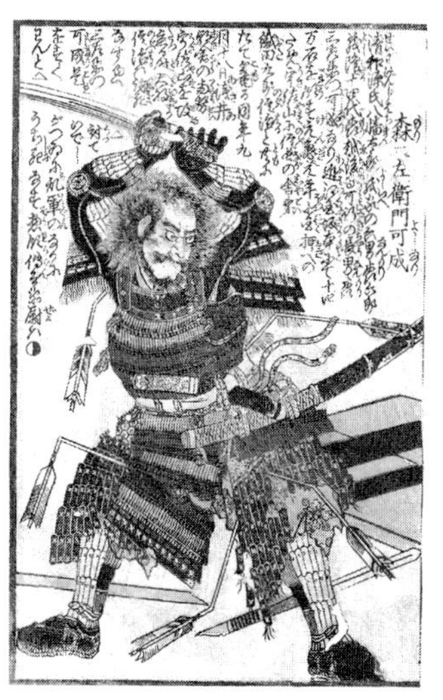

Mori Yoshinari [1523–1570], found on the verso of sheet 15 in volume two [Plate 68], was originally a vassal of the Saitō clan, but when the Saitō were conquered by Oda Nobunaga in 1555, he and his family switched allegiances and his son became Nobunaga's trusted page. Yoshinari died fighting against the Asakura clan in Nobunaga's service.

On the recto of sheet 19 in volume two [Plate 75], the story of Arima Toyouji [1559–1642] is told. One of the longest-lived of all of the heroes, Toyouji was an important figure in

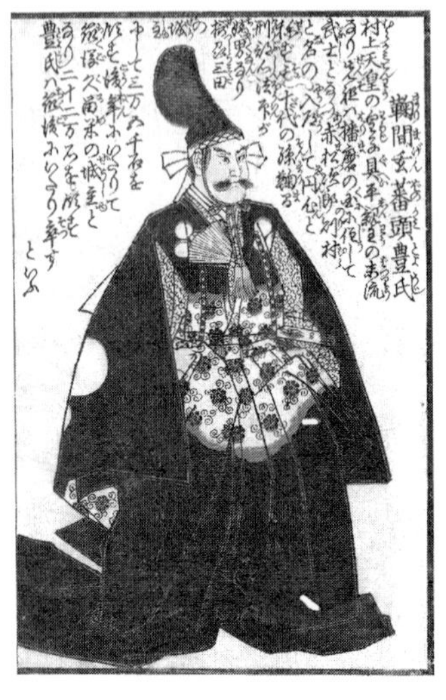

early Edo Japan. He even led an army against the Christians during the Shimabara Rebellion of 1637 to 1638, long after most other leaders from the civil war era had died. Originally a retainer of Hideyoshi Toyotomi, he joined the forces of Tokugawa Ieyasu and fought in the great battle of Sekigahara in 1600. Married to Ieyasu's daughter, he was rewarded handsomely by the Tokugawa throughout his long life.

In volume three, on the recto of sheet 8 [Plate 92], we find Shimazu Yoshihiro [1535–1619]. Both a brilliant general and a canny politician, he was the de facto, if not the de jure, head of the Shimazu clan in Kyushu. When they were defeated by Hideyoshi Toyotomi, he became Hideyoshi's valued vassal and was instrumental in rescuing the remnants of Hideyoshi's armies from Korea in the 1590s when their war against the Ming Chinese ended badly.

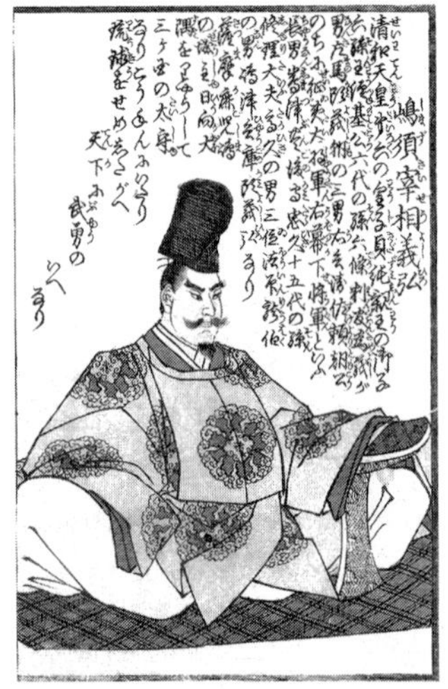

In the great battle of Sekigahara, which fixed the future fate of the feudal order under Tokugawa rule, Yoshihiro led his Shimazu clan, first siding with the eventual victor Tokugawa Ieyasu and then, defeated and humiliated by Torii Mototada, joining with Ishida Mitsunari. When the Ishida side was crushed, Yoshihiro led his clan on a fighting retreat through the huge Tokugawa army and returned to Kyūshū. Because of their bravery in the chaos of war that day, the

Shimazu were allowed to retain their lands under Tokugawa rule, and Yoshihiro himself lived another nineteen years until dying of natural causes. It is said that several of his vassals then followed him in death by committing suicide.

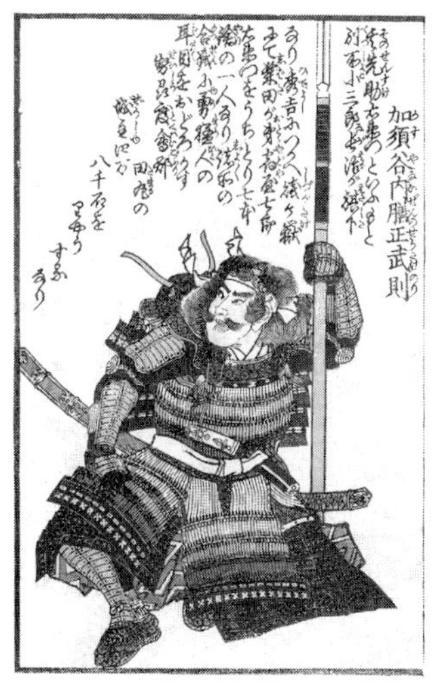

At the recto of page 14 in volume three [Plate 104], we find Kasuya Takenori [1562–1607]. He was an orderly for Hideyoshi and a famous warrior, one of the Seven Spearmen, whose exploits in the great battle of Shizugatake and afterwards in Korea brought him the castle of Kakogawa in Harima. Though relatively minor in status, he was well known and respected for his valor. Takenori joined the "western army" of Ishida Mitsunari at the battle of Sekigahara against the Tokugawa and was defeated. He lost his holdings but was granted a small fief under the Tokugawa after all; however, with his death his clan disappeared from the pages of history.

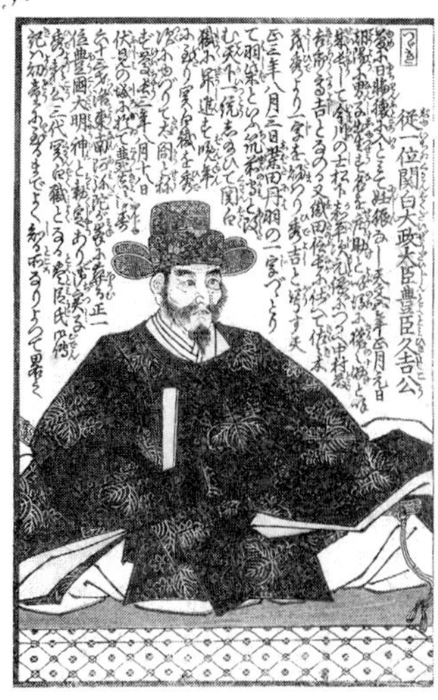

The last page of the final volume of the series [Plate 117], interestingly, ends not with Tokugawa Ieyasu, the founder of the ruling clan and victor of the civil wars, but rather with Hideyoshi Toyotomi [1536–1598]. The son of a peasant foot soldier, he rose through the ranks under the first great unifier, Oda Nobunaga. After Oda's assassination at the hands of a treacherous vassal, Hideyoshi arose as the greatest military power of his time. A crafty political figure, he balanced and neutralized competing clans, keeping himself in control of a coalition that included the Tokugawa clan, among other powers.

Hideyoshi's ruinous invasion of Ming China through Korea weakened the clan, and his early death left his unprepared son, Hideyori, as clan head. A mere two years after his death, the battle of Sekigahara pitted the western clans against those from the east. The defeat of the west left the Hideyoshi clan in control of the domain of Osaka but little else, and the Tokugawa gained control of Japan. The clan would be utterly destroyed fifteen years later, when the Tokugawa army burned Ōsaka Castle after a long seige.

These eight are just a few examples of the great generals, clan heads, and heroic warriors that populate the pages of this precis of the Warring States epoch. Some died young in battle, some lived long lives, some were disgraced, some honored, and some both. The dominant theme is change of status, of fortune, of great success and arbitrary failure—not the message normal to the authoritarian culture the Tokugawa had always controlled.

It was in the general interest of the artists, writers, and publishers to produce material that would be popular and sell copies. The Tokugawa had always kept strict control of publishing, both of prints and books, via a system of censors. Could it be that as the end of the old regime approached, forms of tacit rebellion against the status quo made the long-ended civil wars a popular topic? The fact that the very last "hero" is not Tokugawa Ieyasu but rather Hideyoshi Toyotomi might point in that direction.

A long-sanctioned art form, the "warrior images," combined with the revitalized scholarship of the late Edo period outside of government control, and a groundswell of interest in the bloody and turbulent civil wars that created the peaceful and stagnant present crumbling in the 1860s, created these little books. Dover has breathed new life into them with their republication.

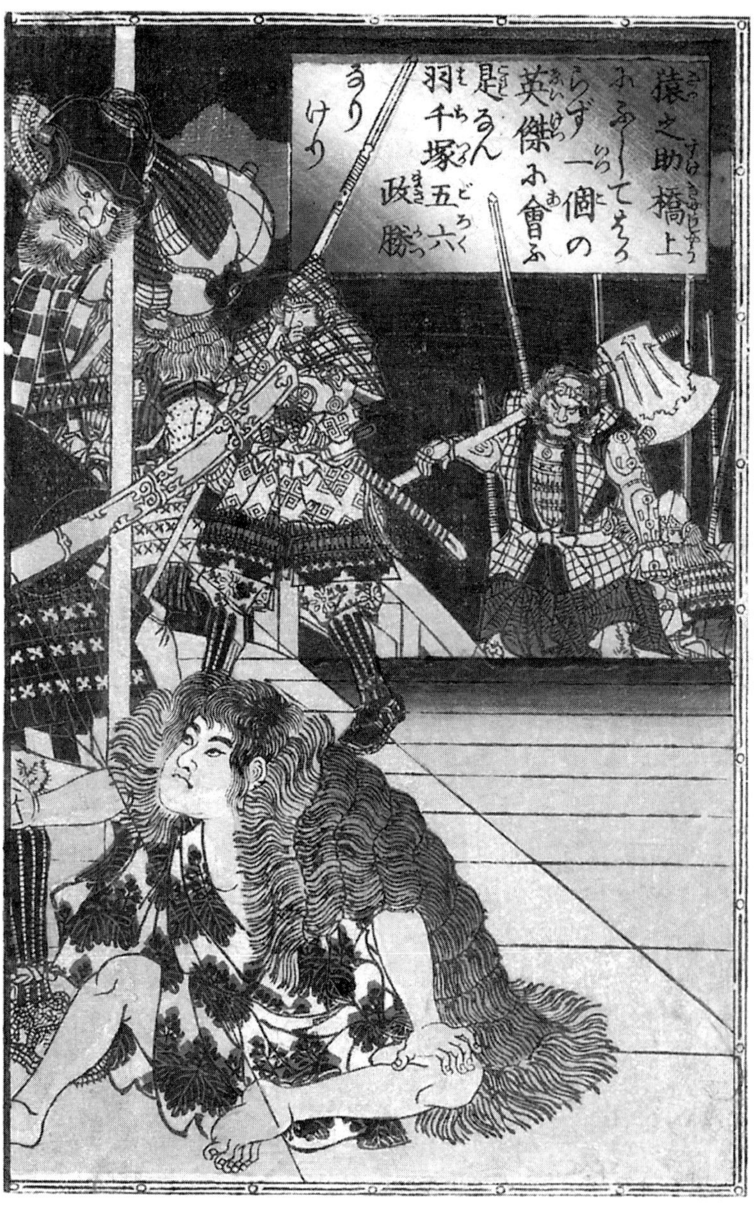

PLATE 1

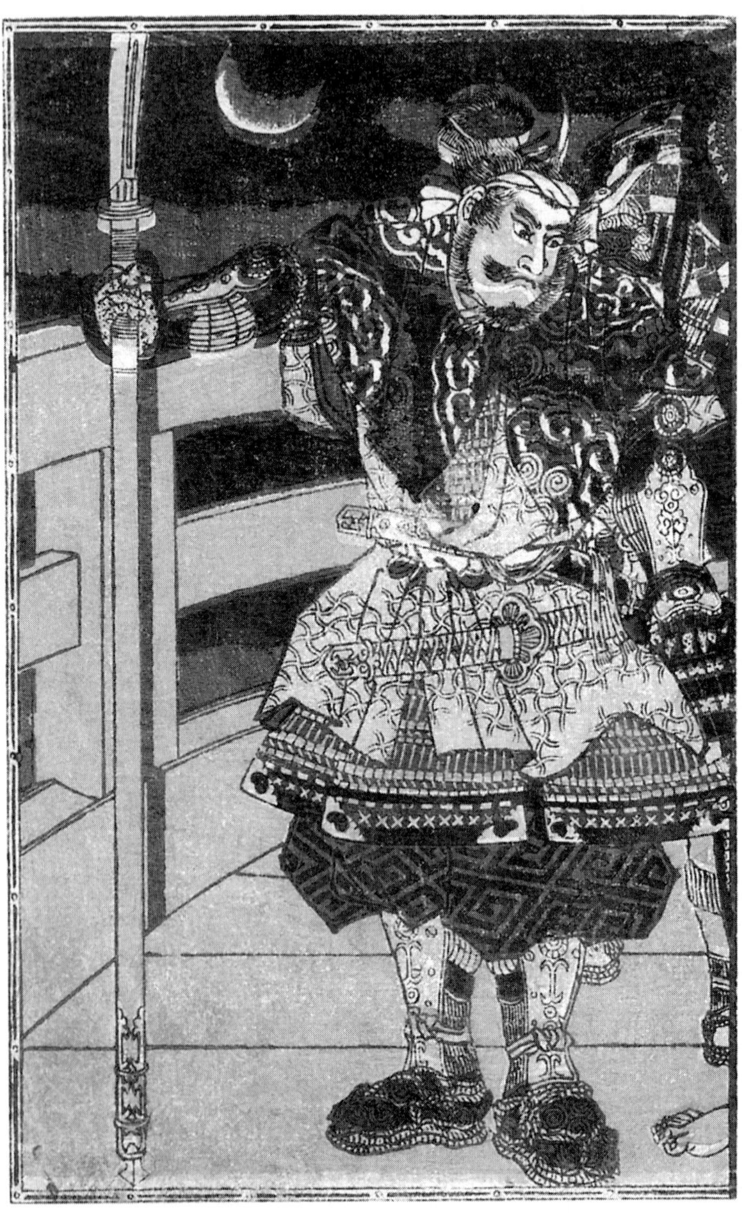

Plate 2

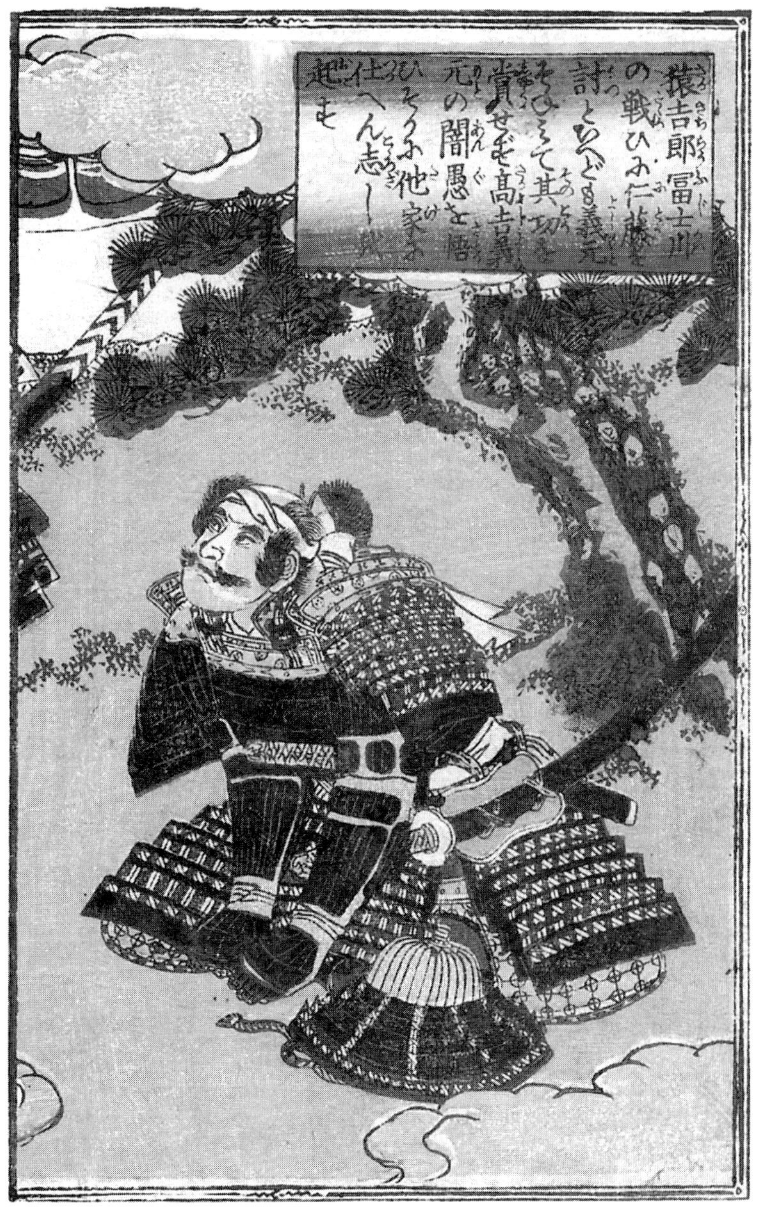
猿吉郎冨士川
の戦ひに仁藤を
討とるといへども義元
そねみて其功を
賞せず高吉義
元の闇愚を悟
ひそかに他家に
仕へん志し
起す

Plate 3

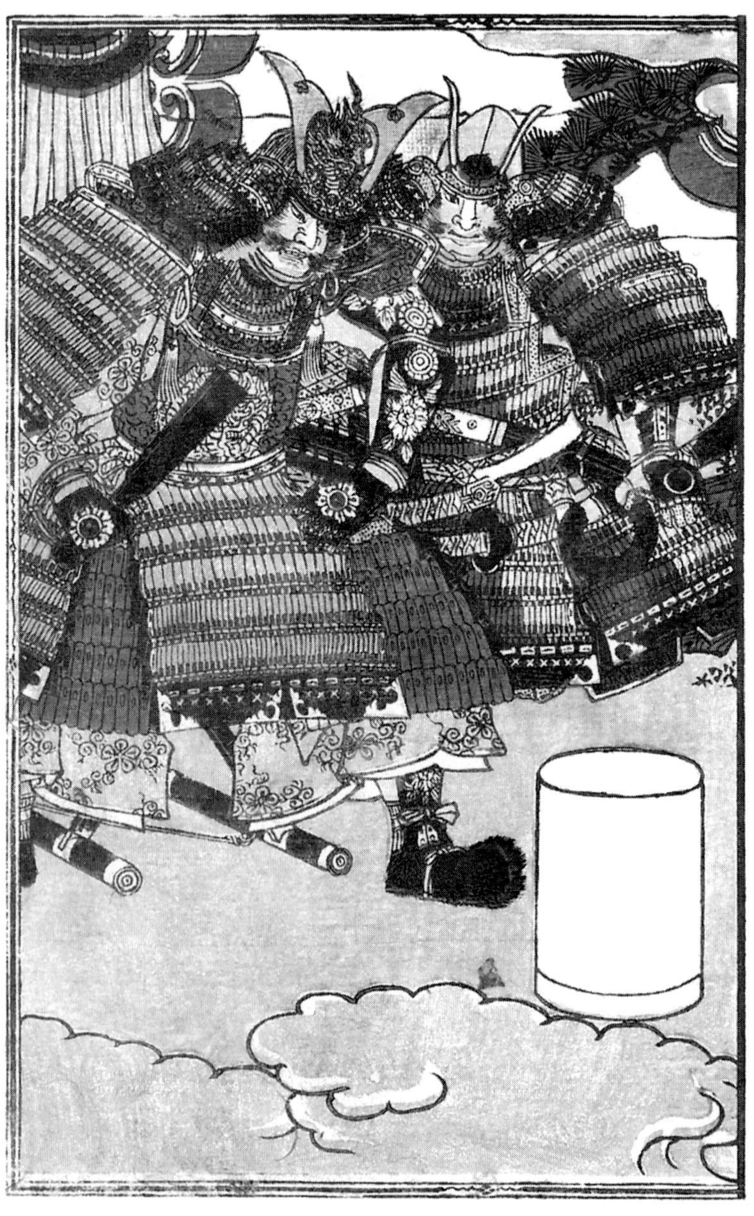

Plate 4

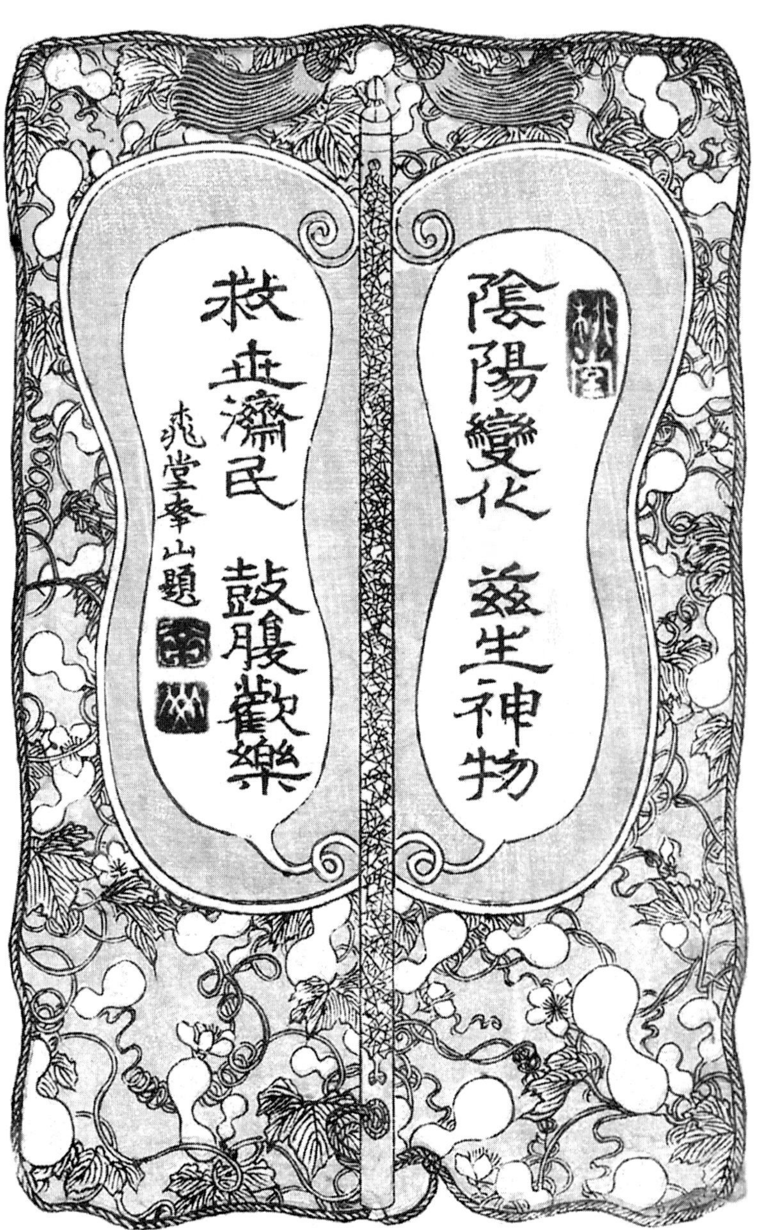

Plate 5

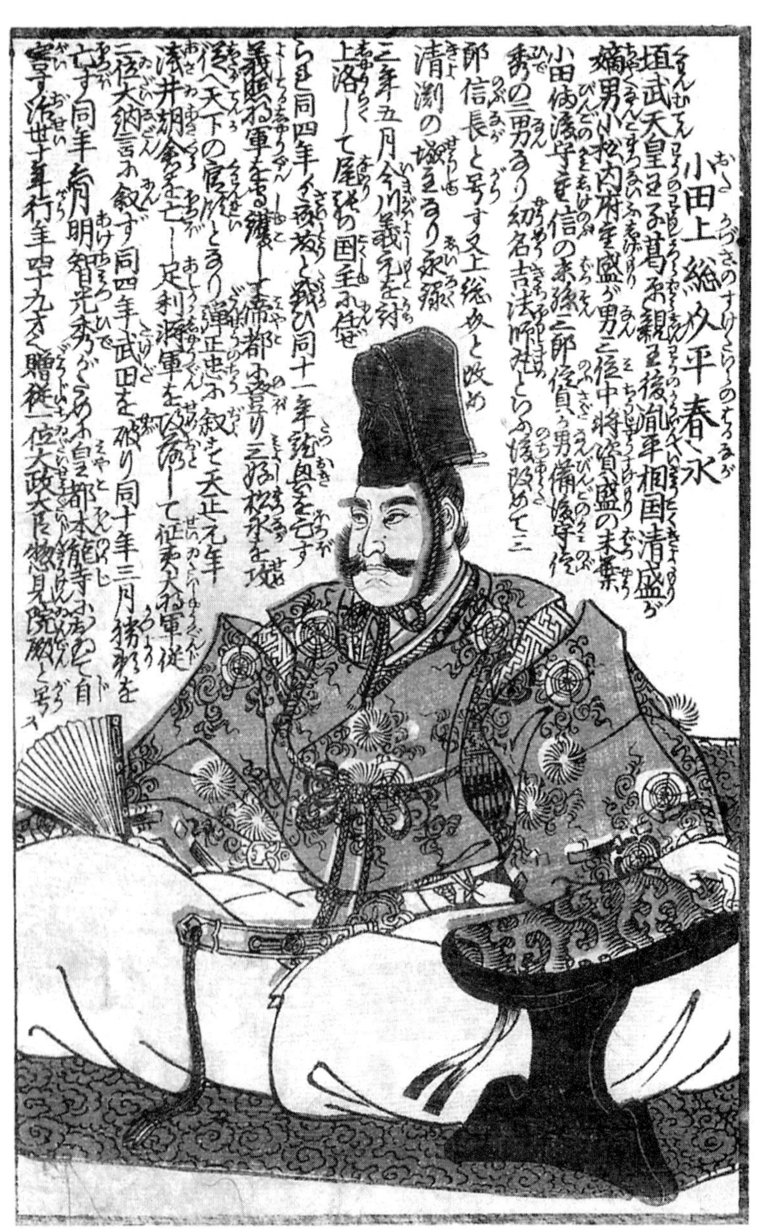

PLATE 6

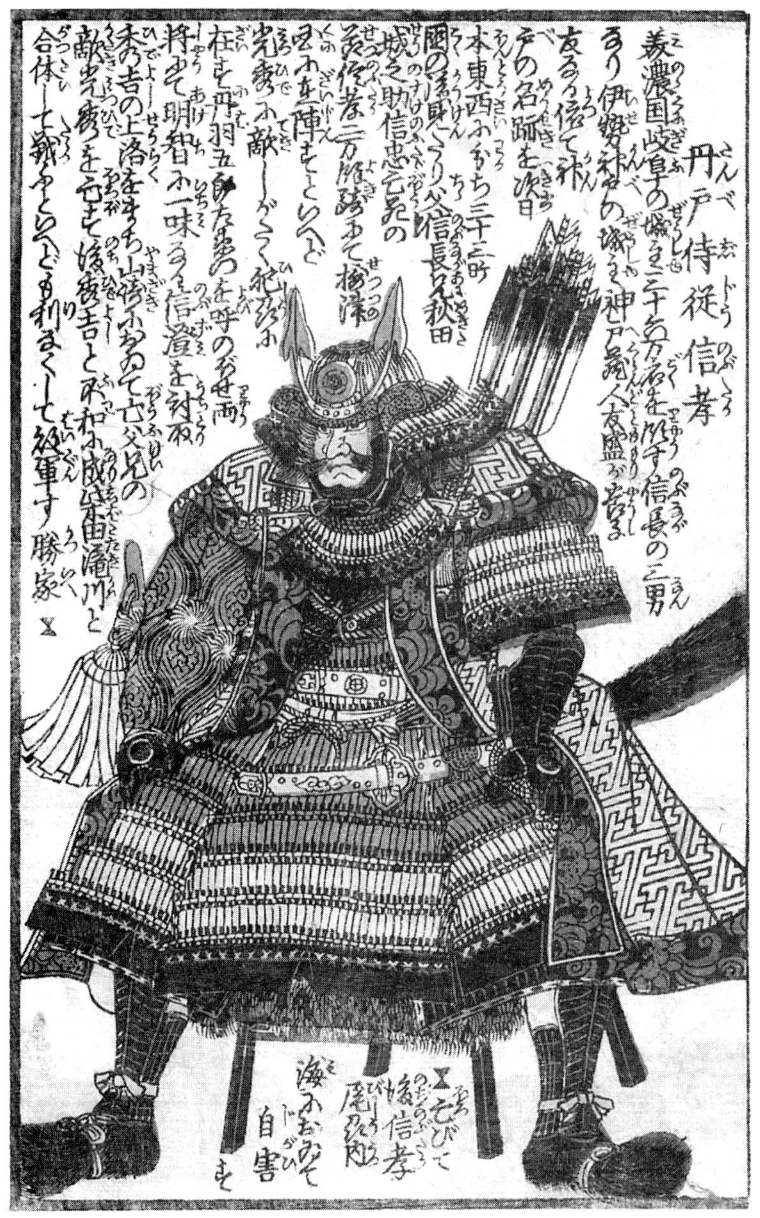

Plate 7

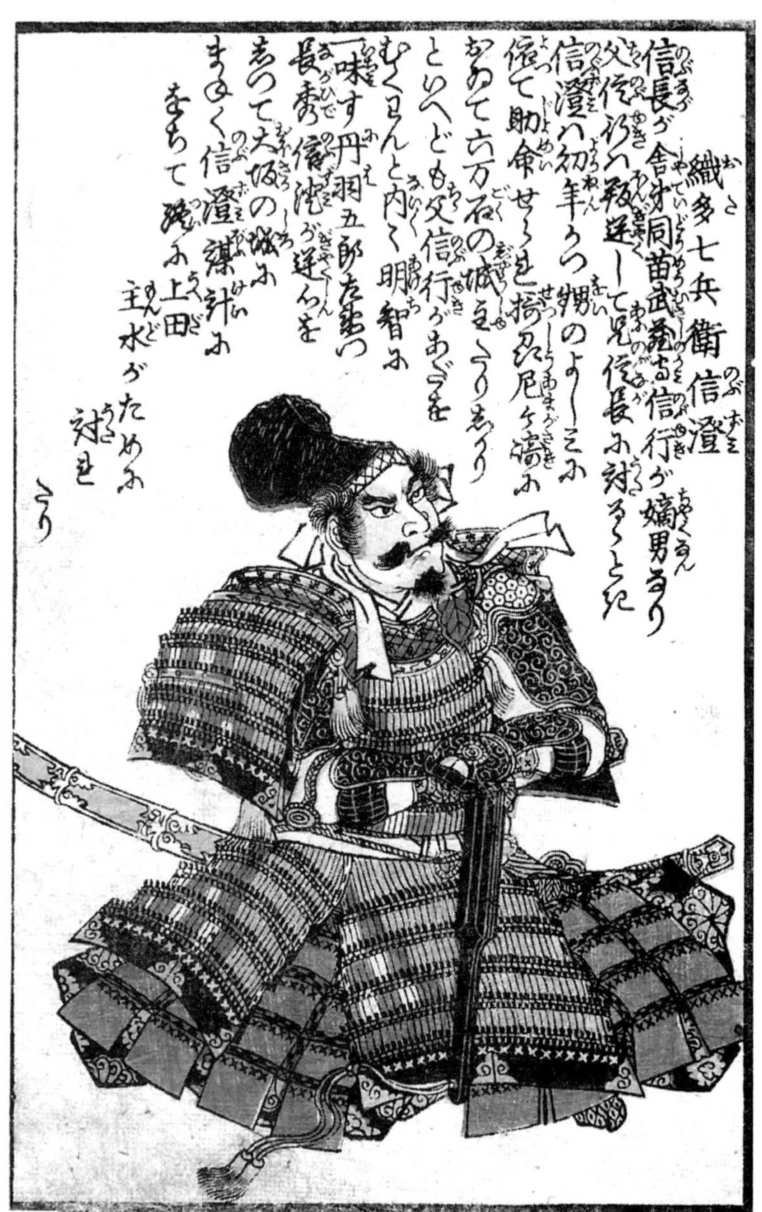

PLATE 8

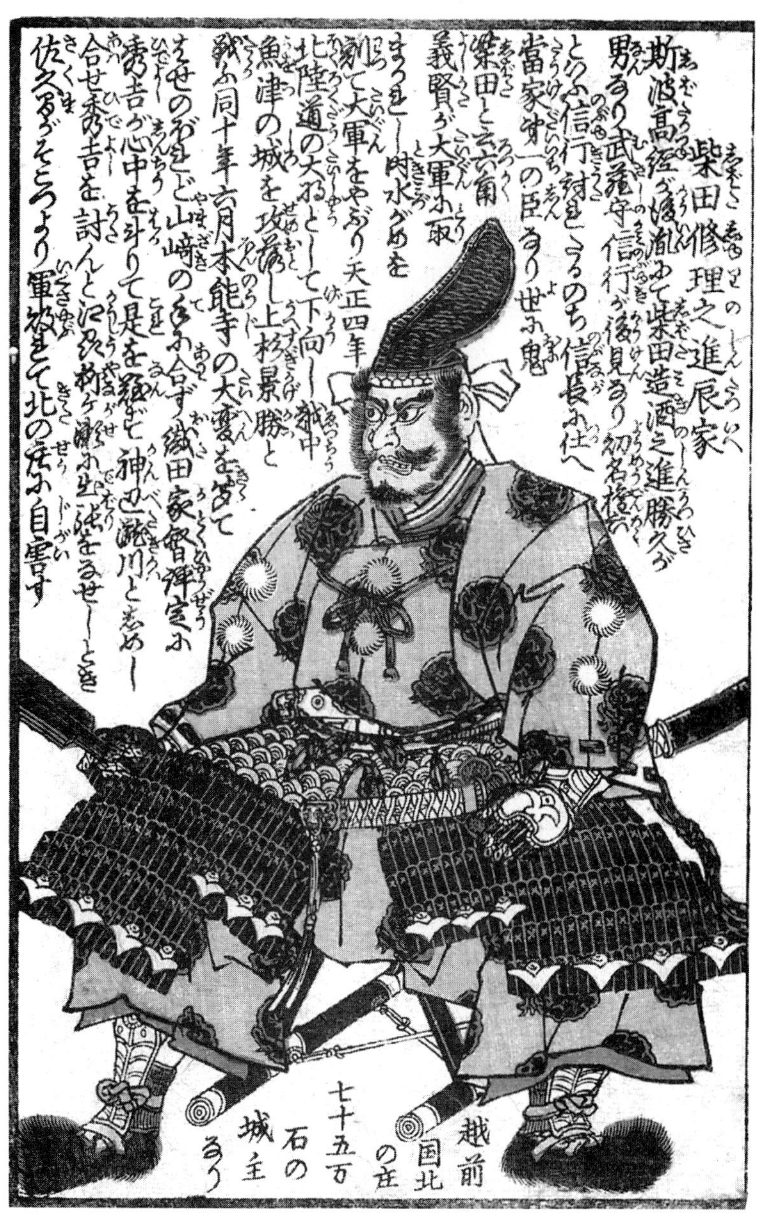

柴田修理之進辰家
斯波高経が後胤にて柴田造酒之進勝久が
男なり武蔵守信行が後見なり初名権六
といふ信行討れしのち信長に仕へ
当家第一の臣なり世に鬼
柴田と云六角
義賢が大軍に取
まかれし時水がめを
割て大軍をやぶり天正四年
北陸道の大将として下向し越中
魚津の城を攻落し上杉景勝と
戦ふ同十年六月本能寺の大変をきゝて
合せ秀吉を討んと江北柳ケ瀬に出張をなせしとき
佐久間がそこなひより軍敗れて北の庄に自害す
越前国北の庄
七十五万石の城主なり

PLATE 9

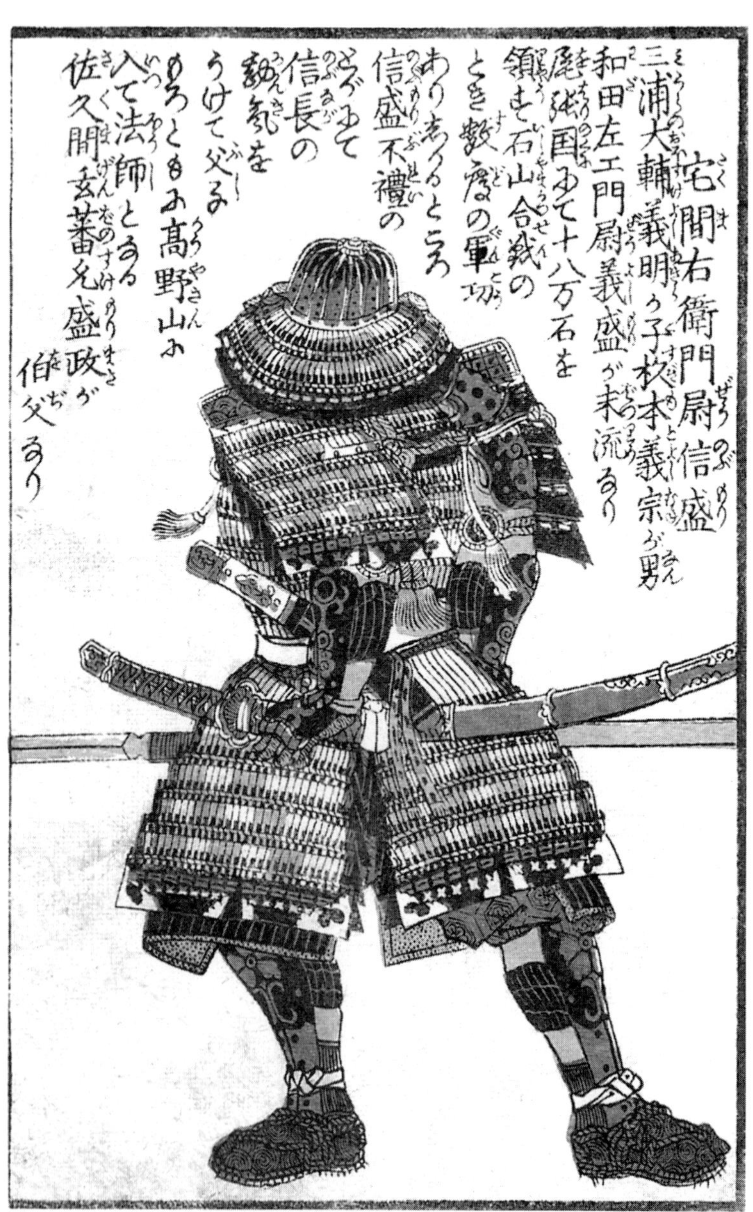
宅間右衛門尉信盛
三浦大輔義明が子杉本義宗が男
和田左エ門尉義盛が末流なり
尾張国にて十八万石を
領す石山合戦の
とき数度の軍功
ありしかところ
信盛不禮の
ことにて
信長の
勘気を
うけて父子
ともに高野山に
入て法師となる
佐久間玄蕃允盛政が
伯父なり

PLATE 10

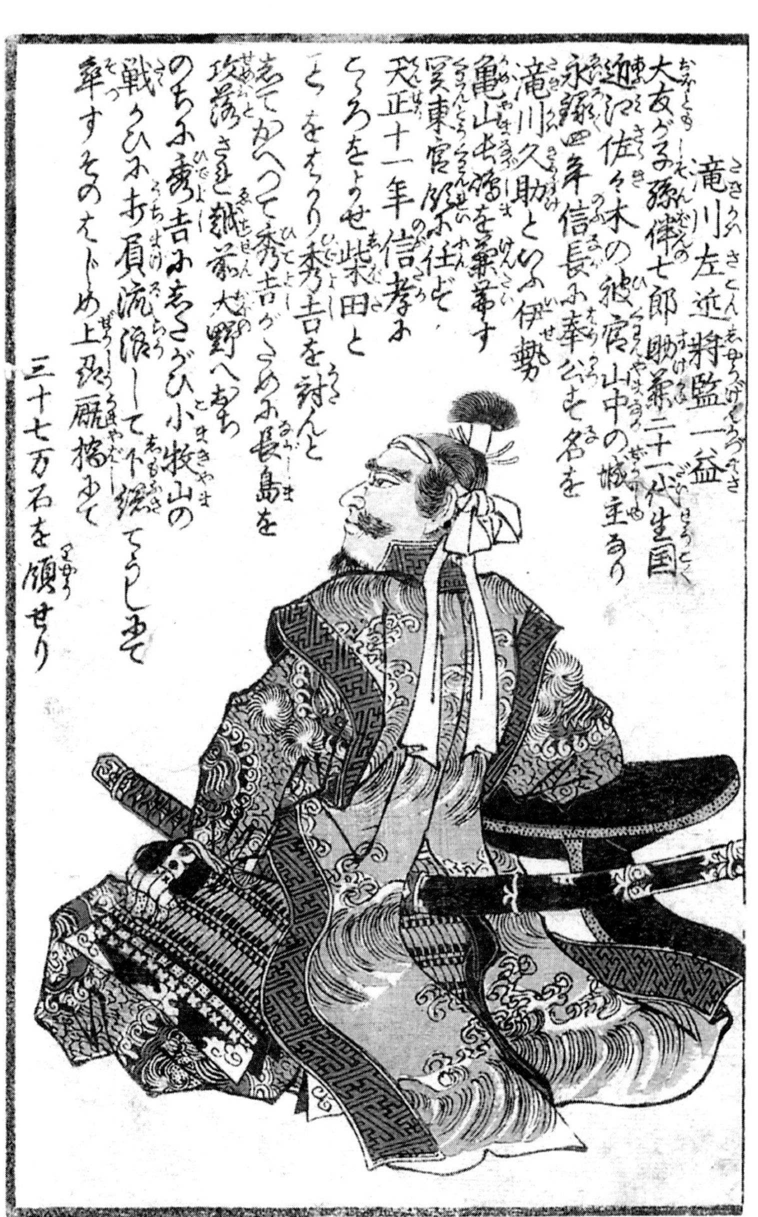

PLATE 11

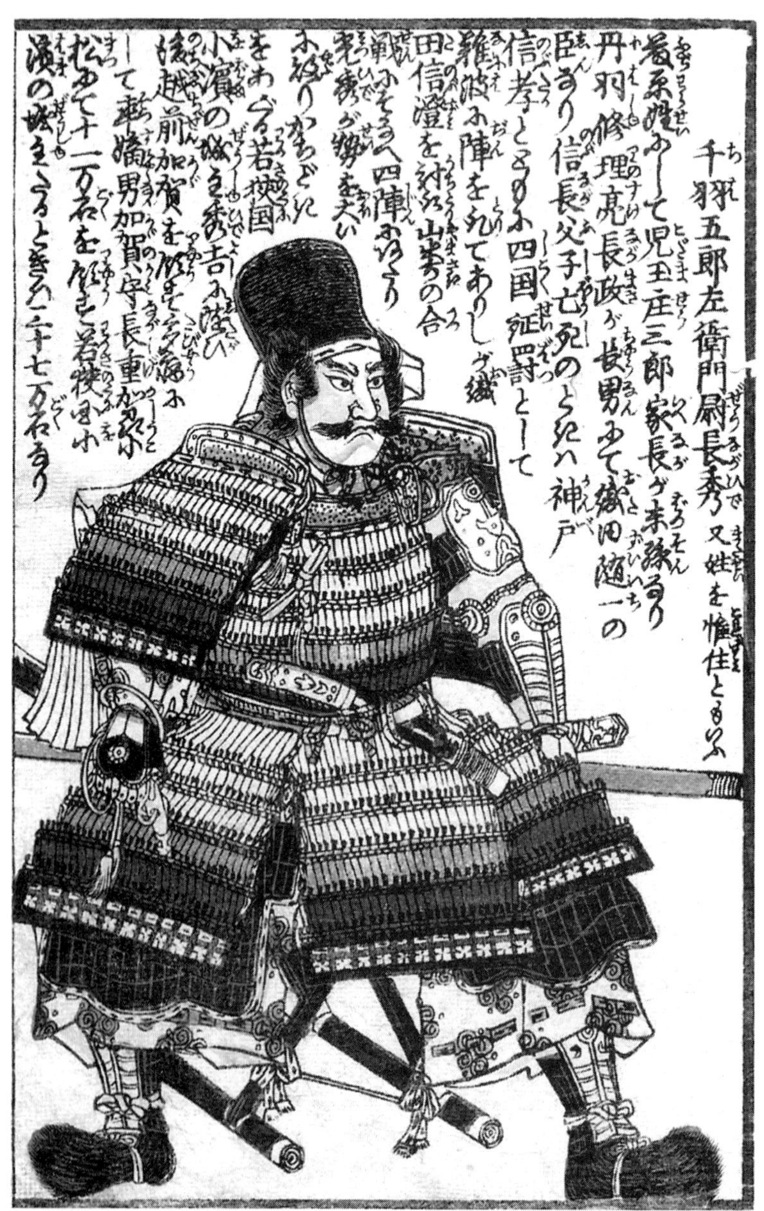

PLATE 12

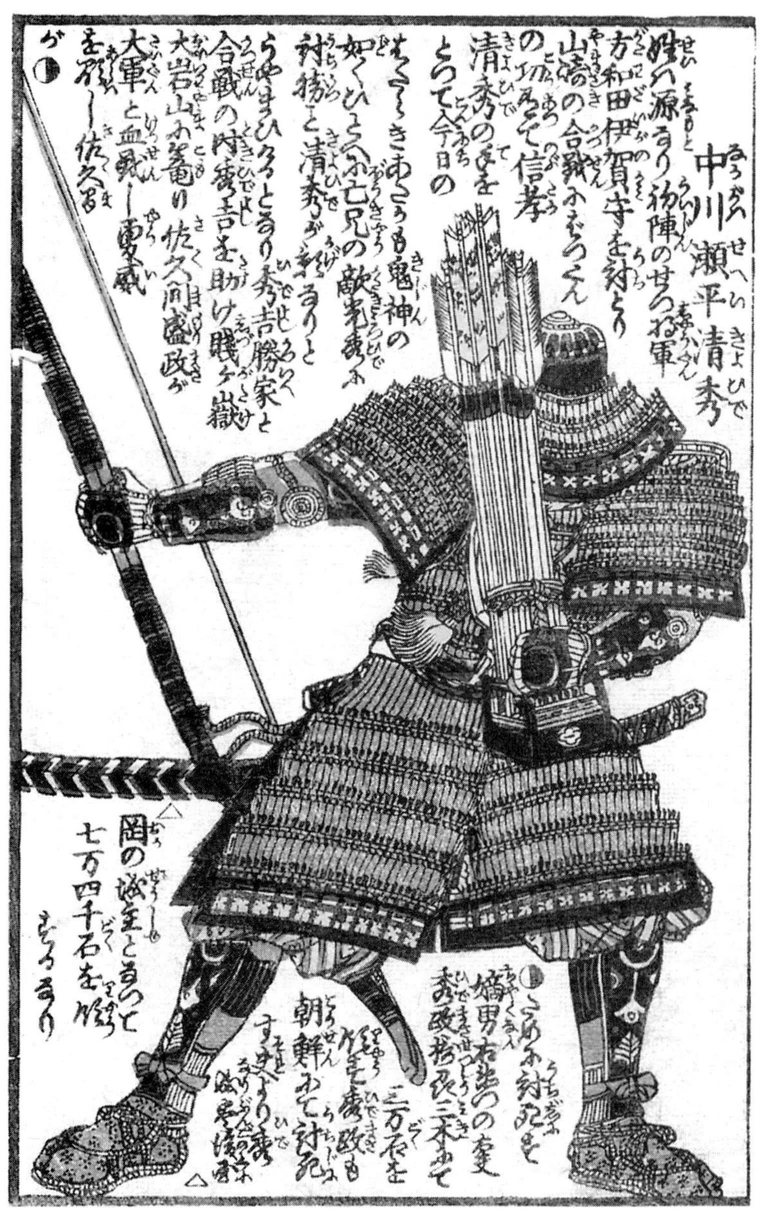

PLATE 13

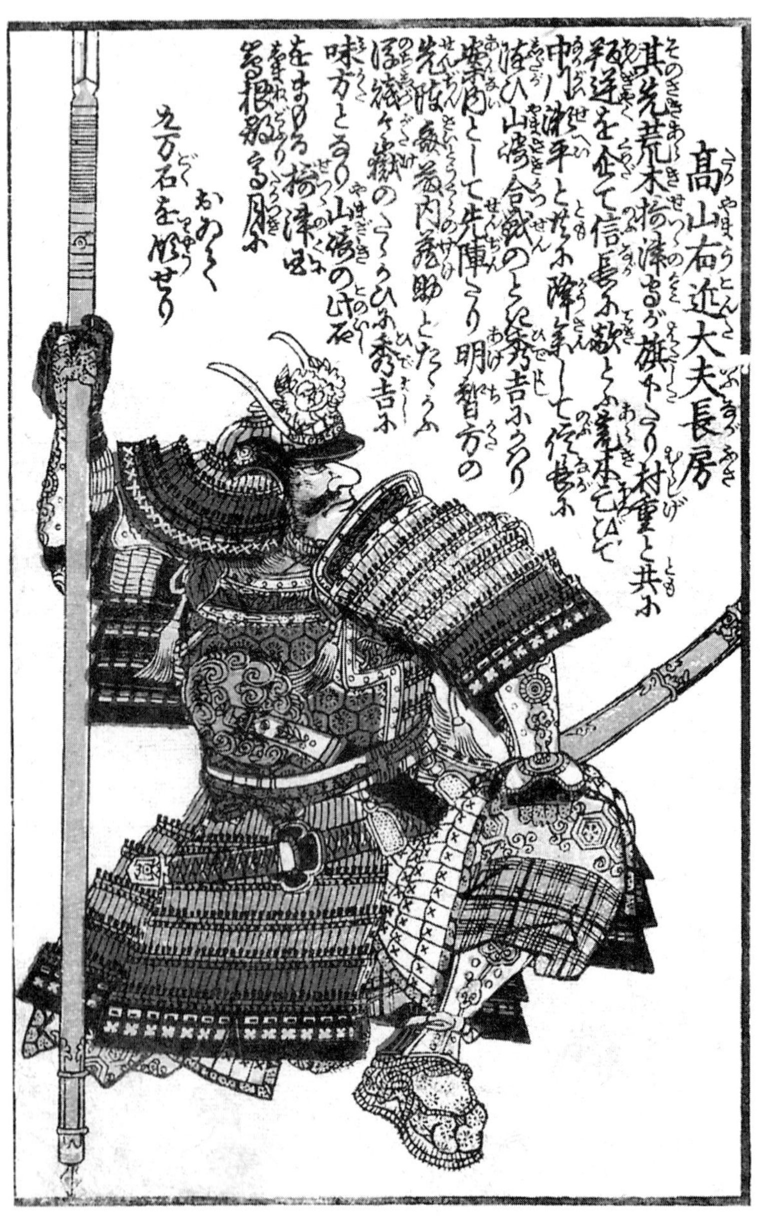

PLATE 14

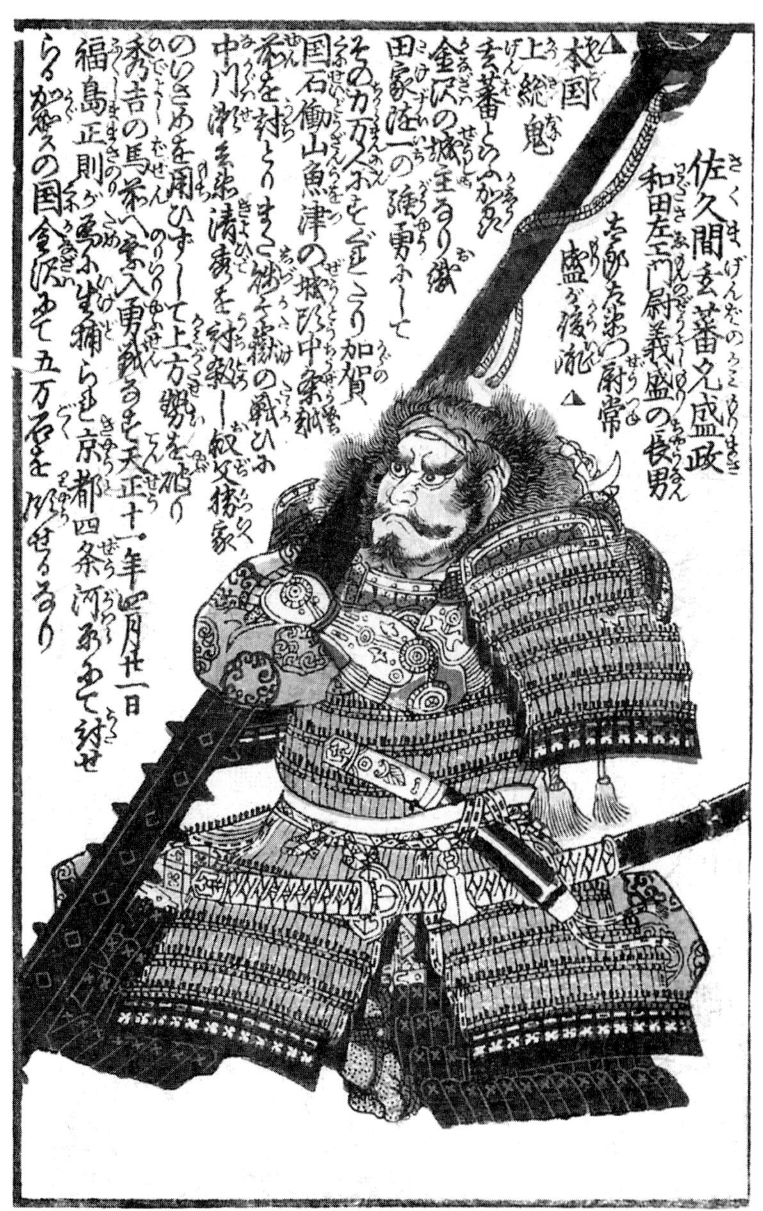

Plate 15

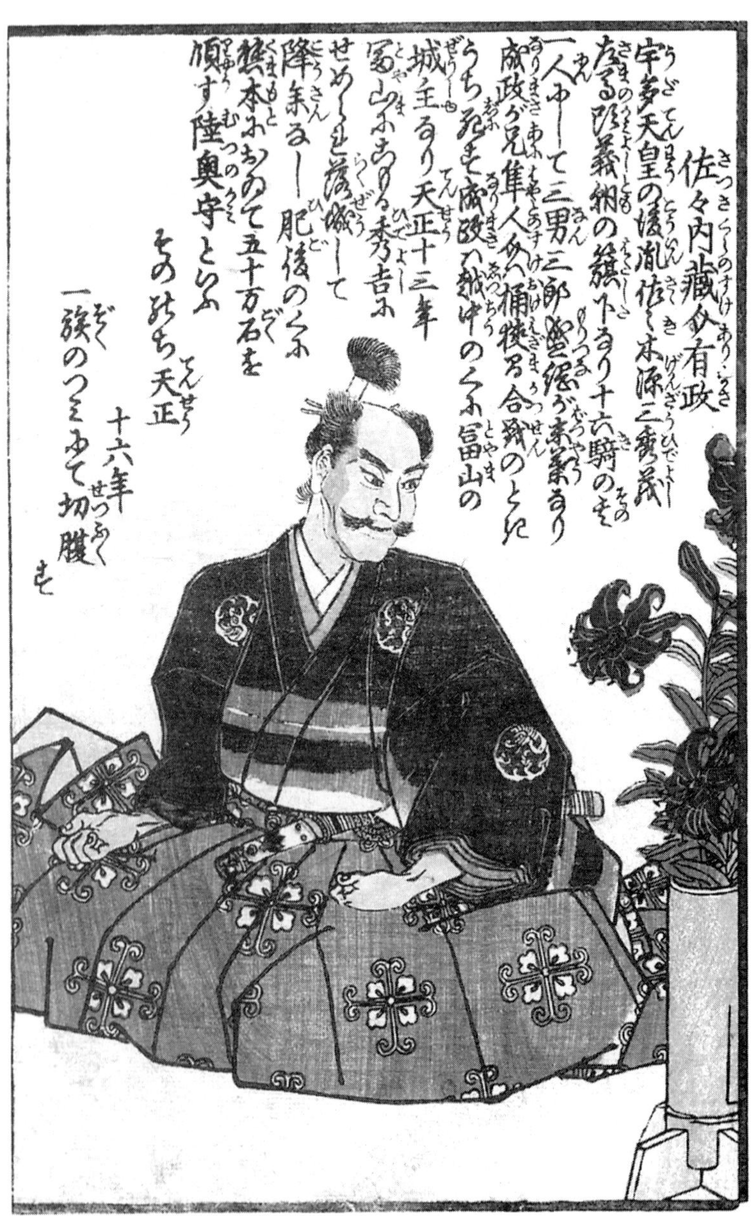

Plate 16

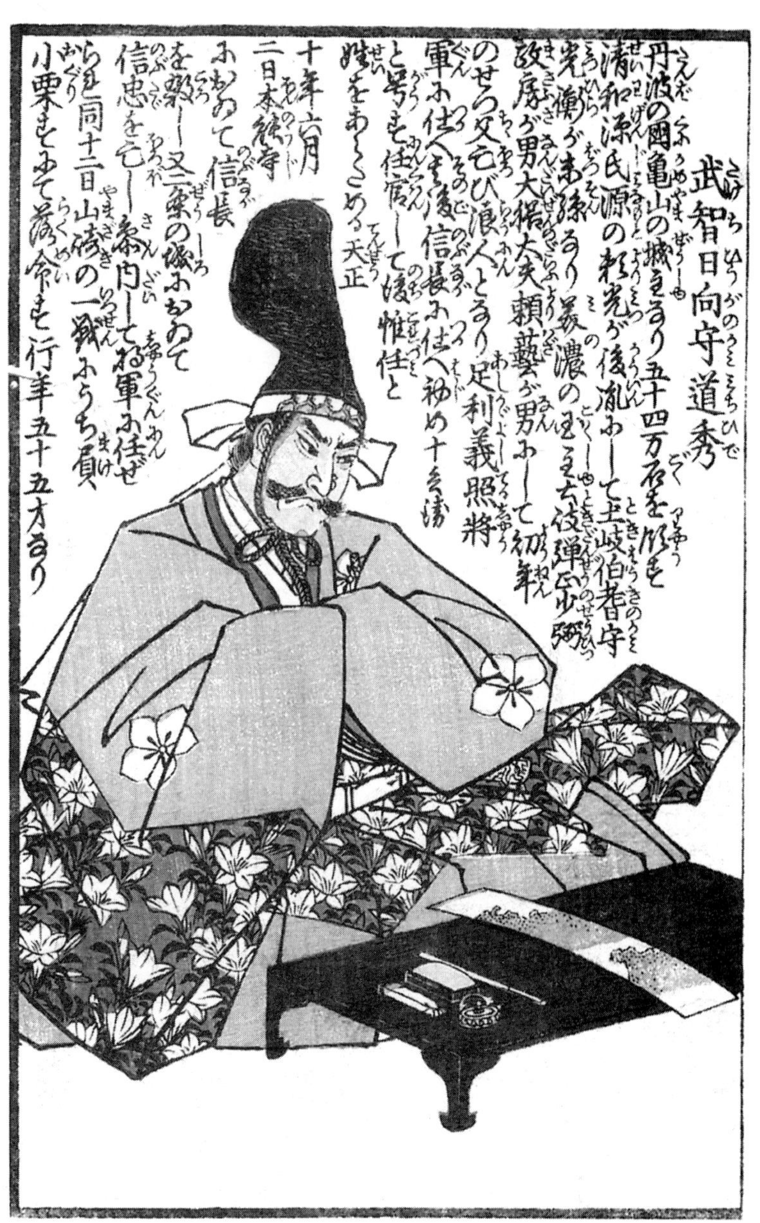

PLATE 17

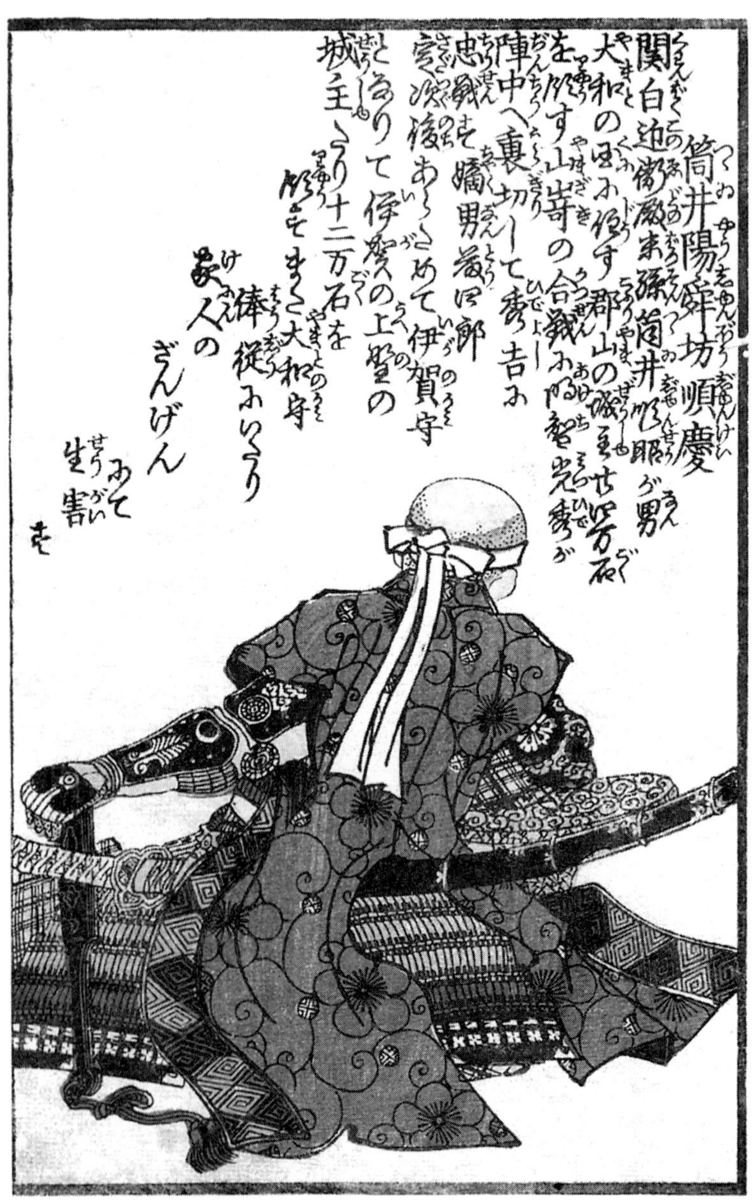

Plate 18

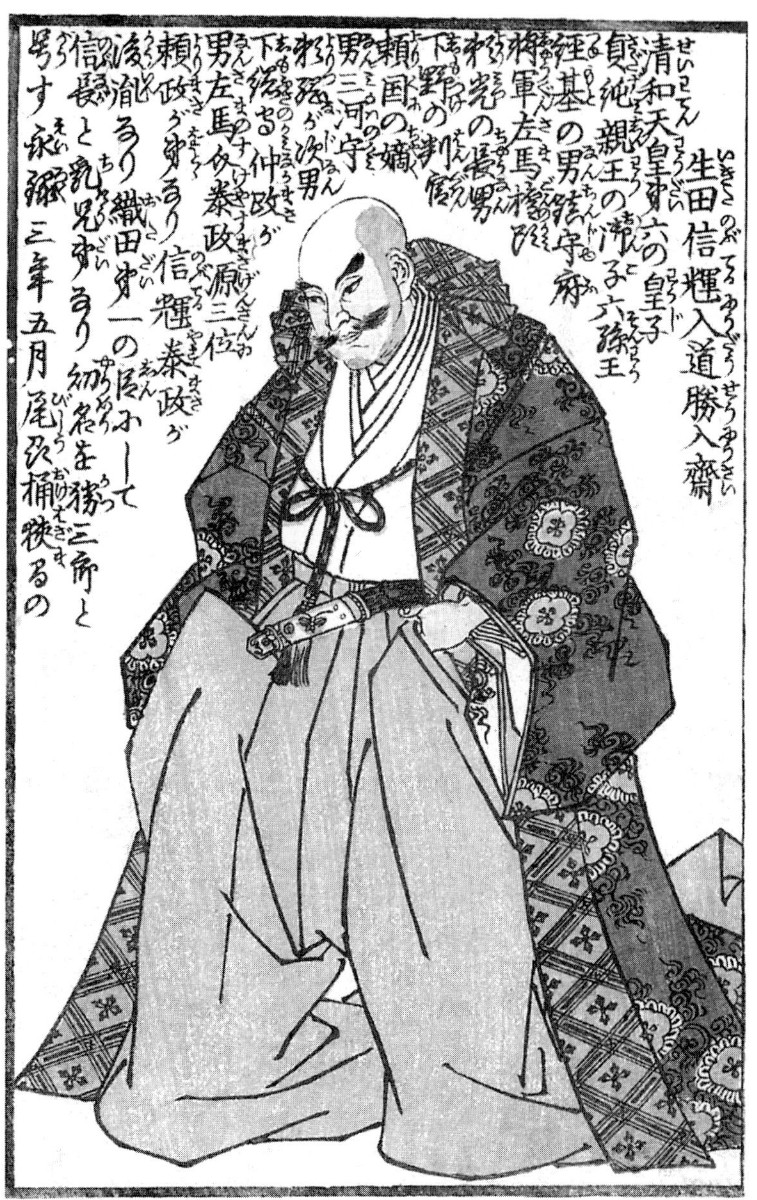

PLATE 19

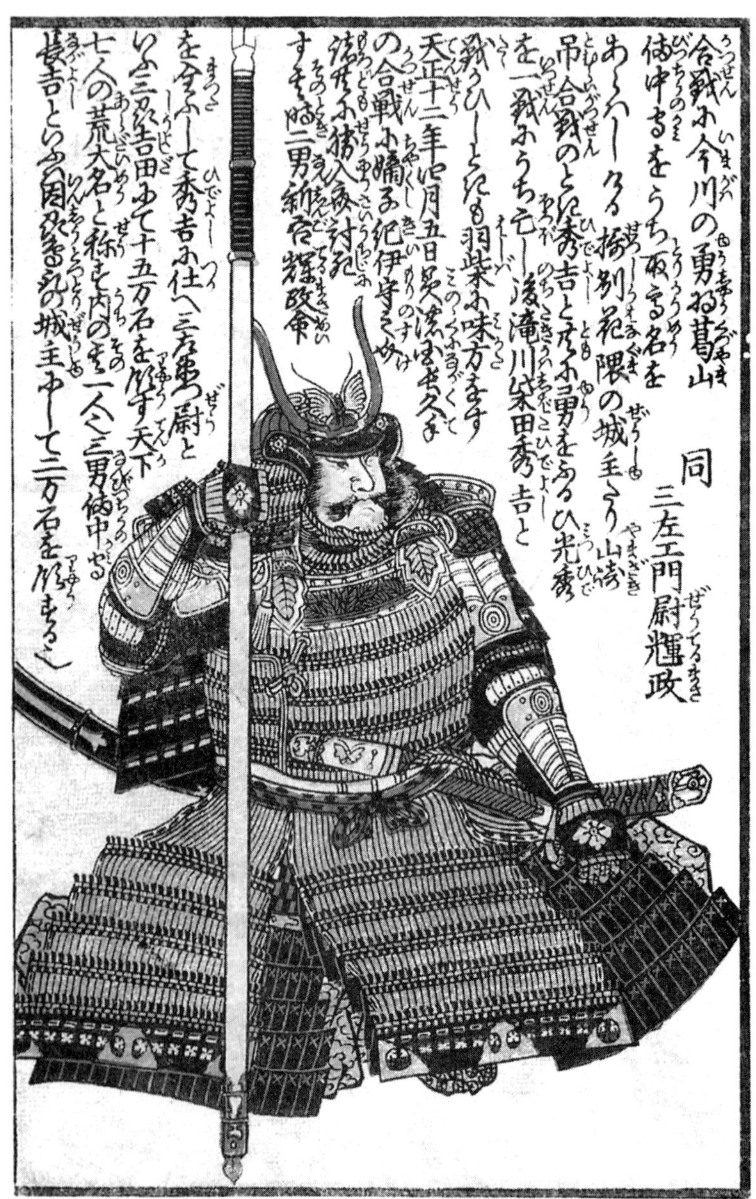

Plate 20

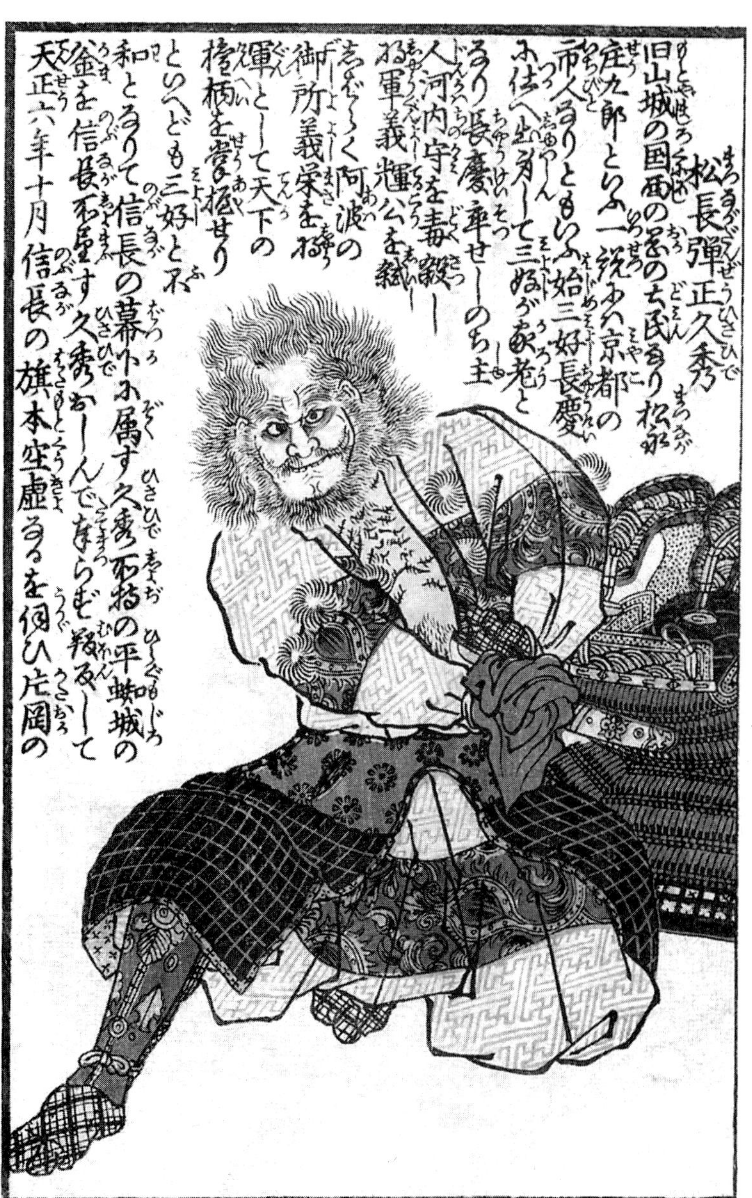

PLATE 21

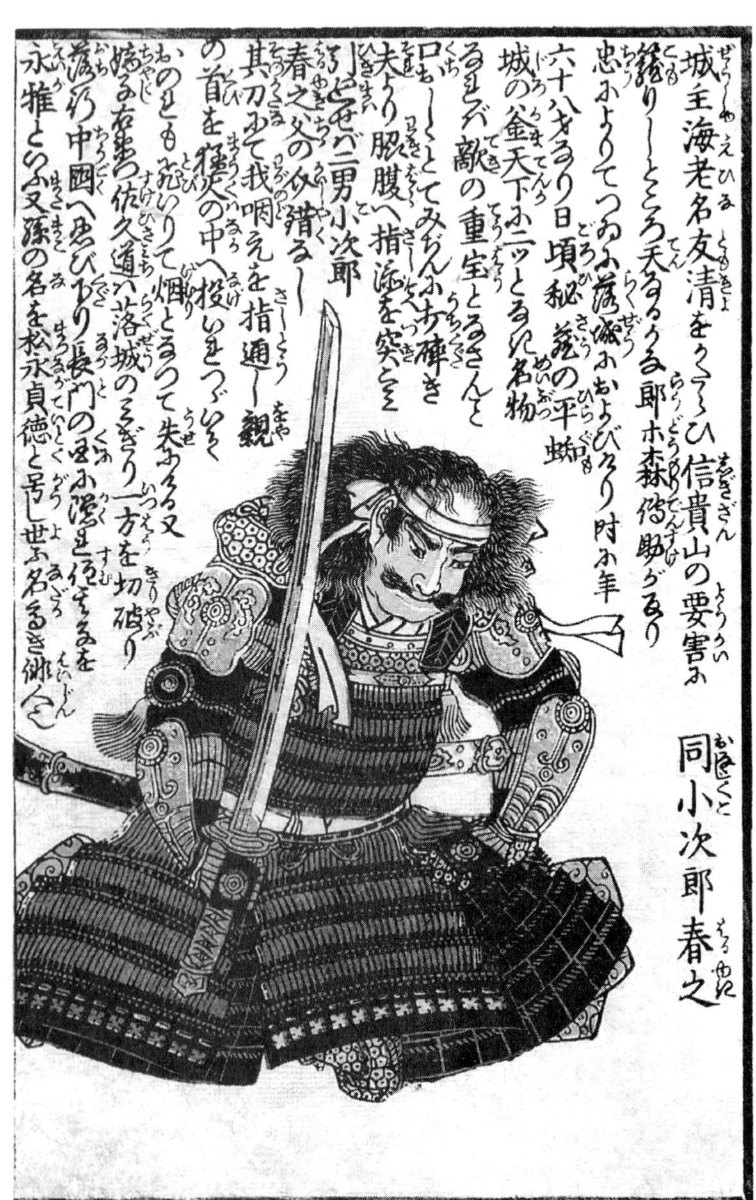

Plate 22

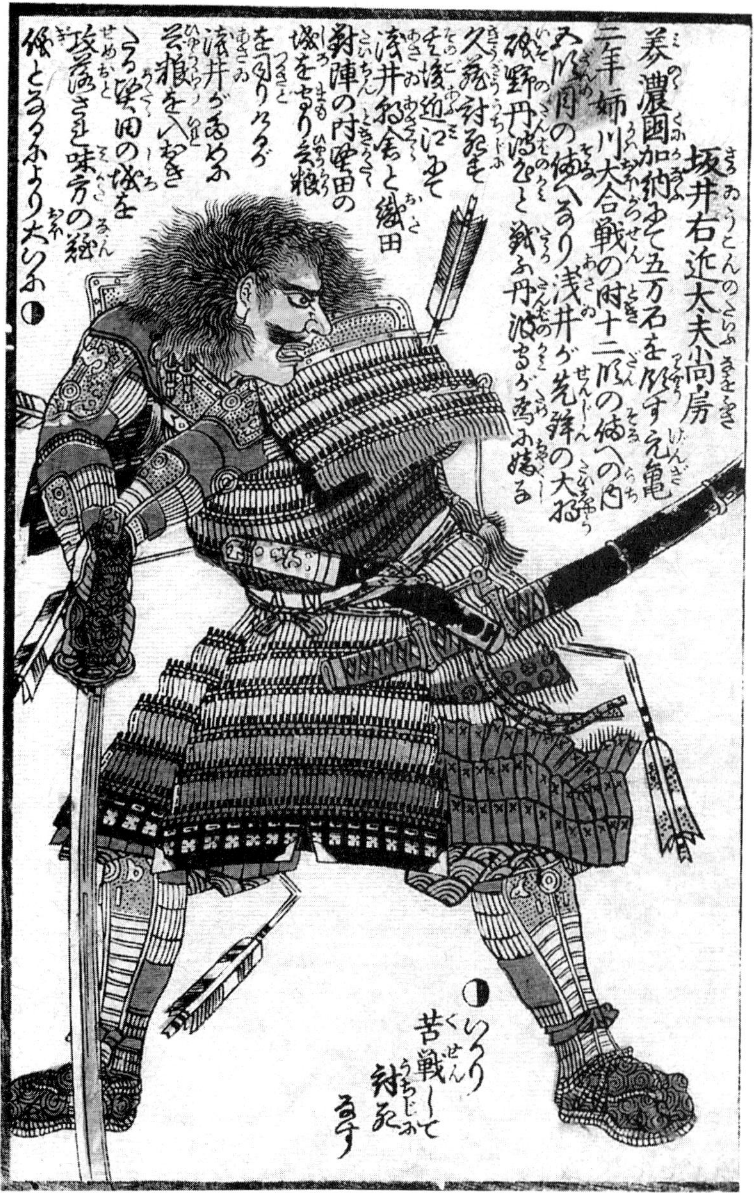

Plate 23

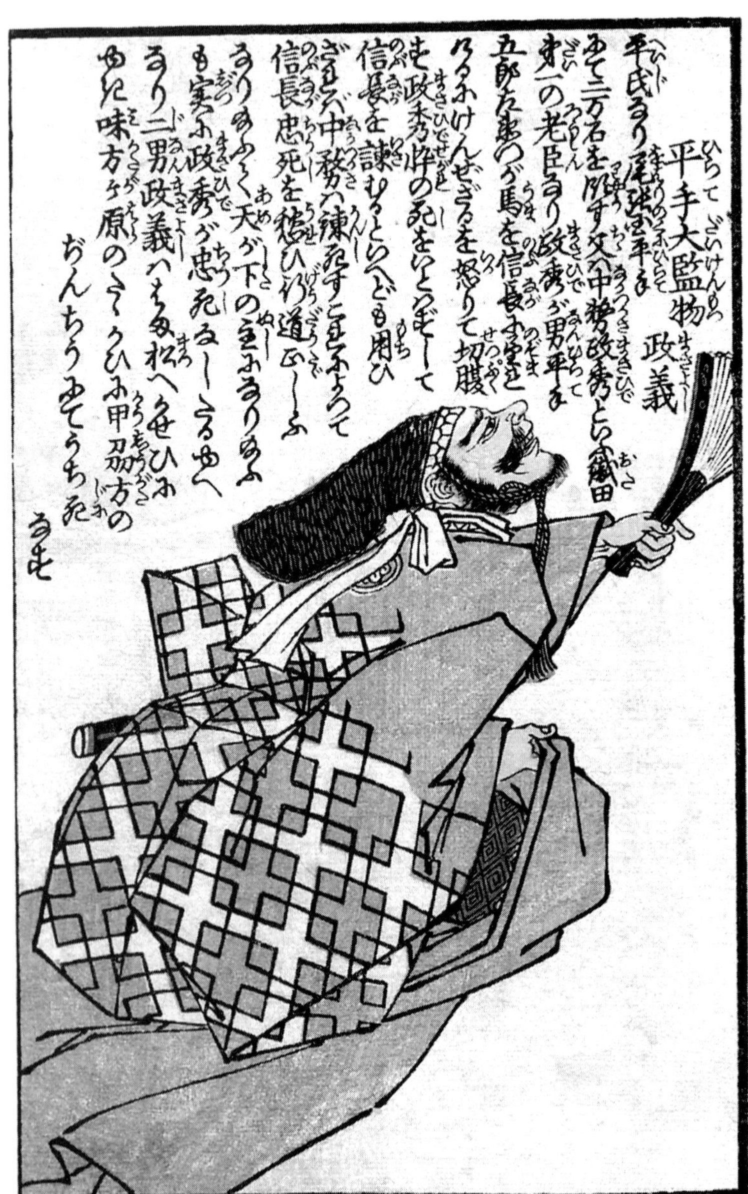

PLATE 24

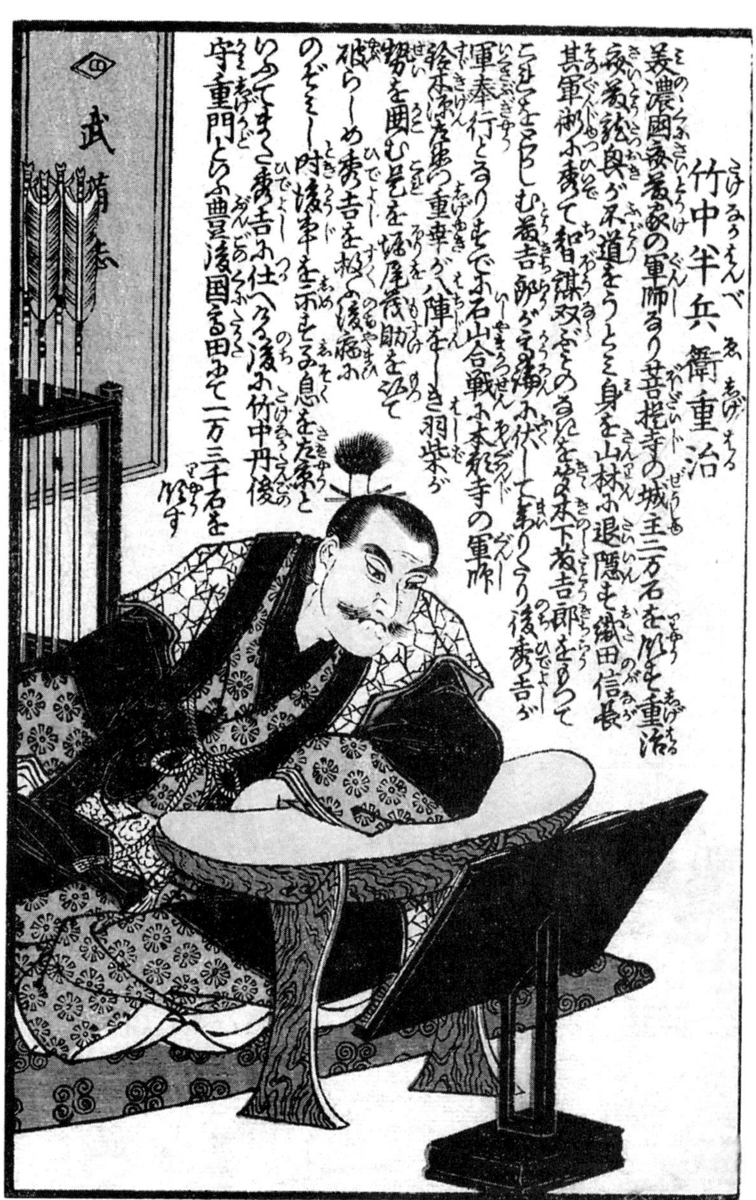

PLATE 25

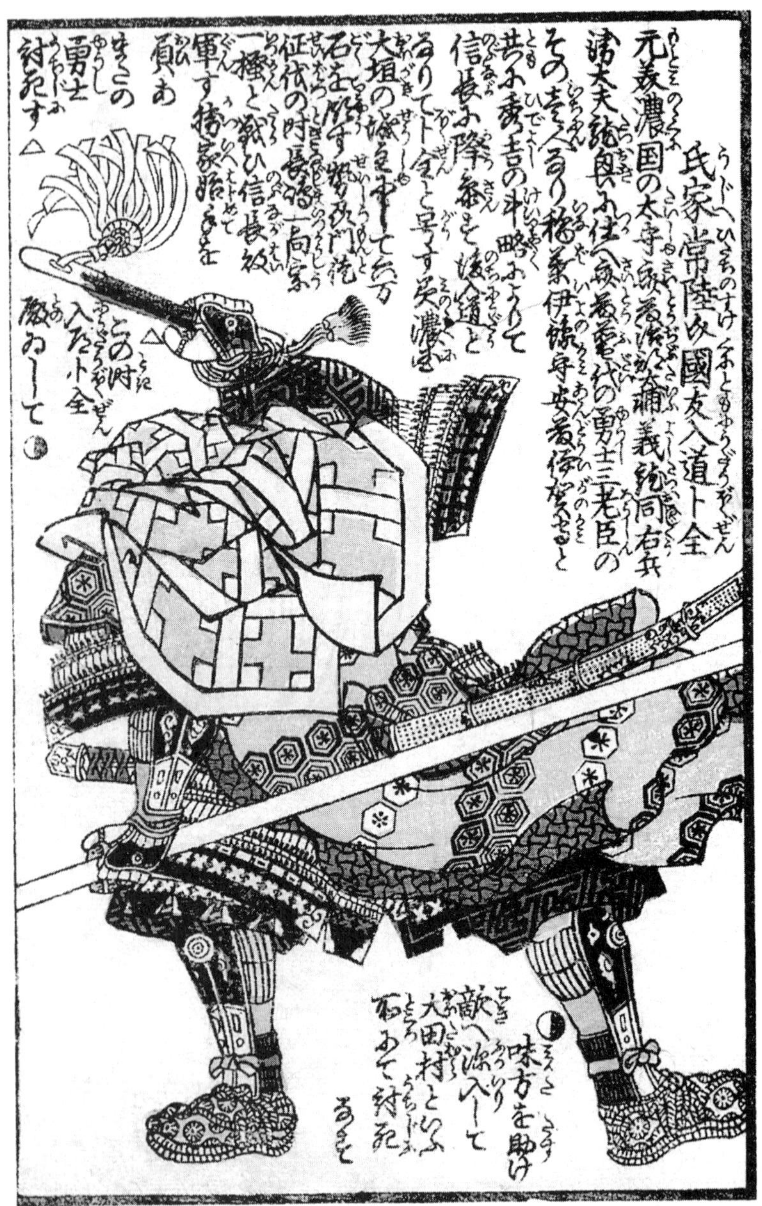

PLATE 26

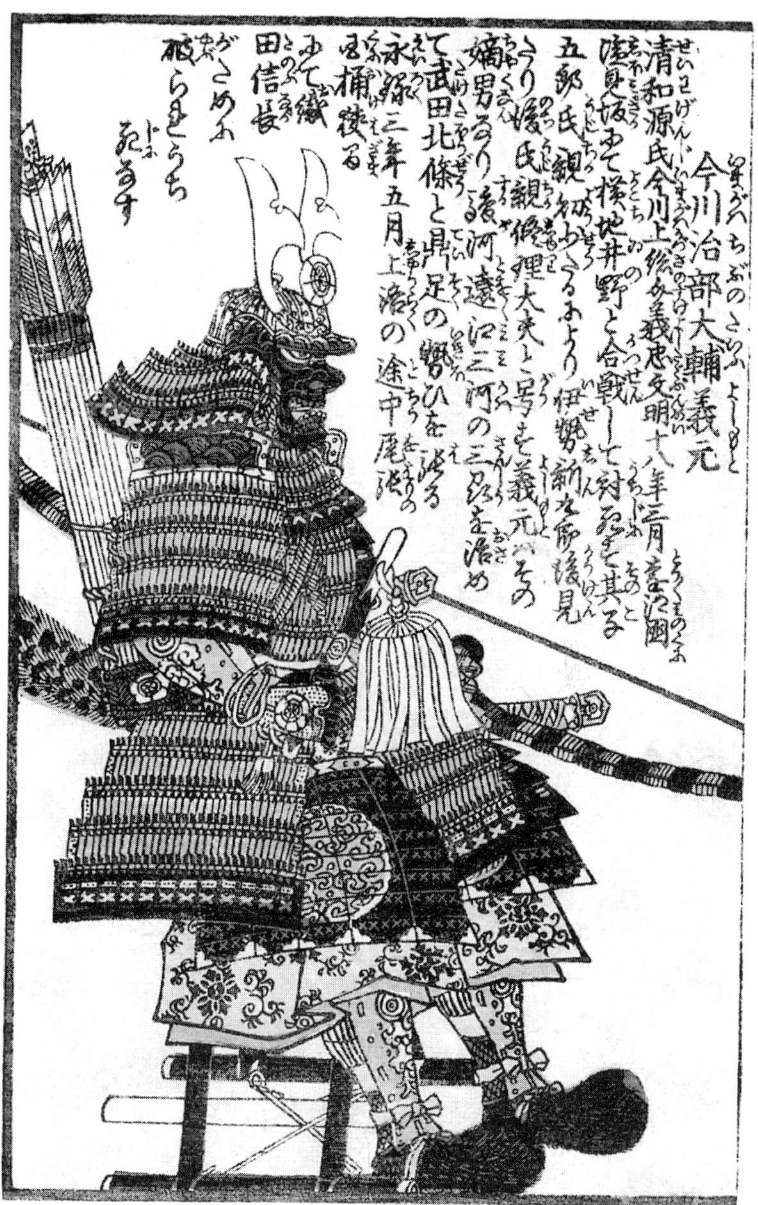

PLATE 27

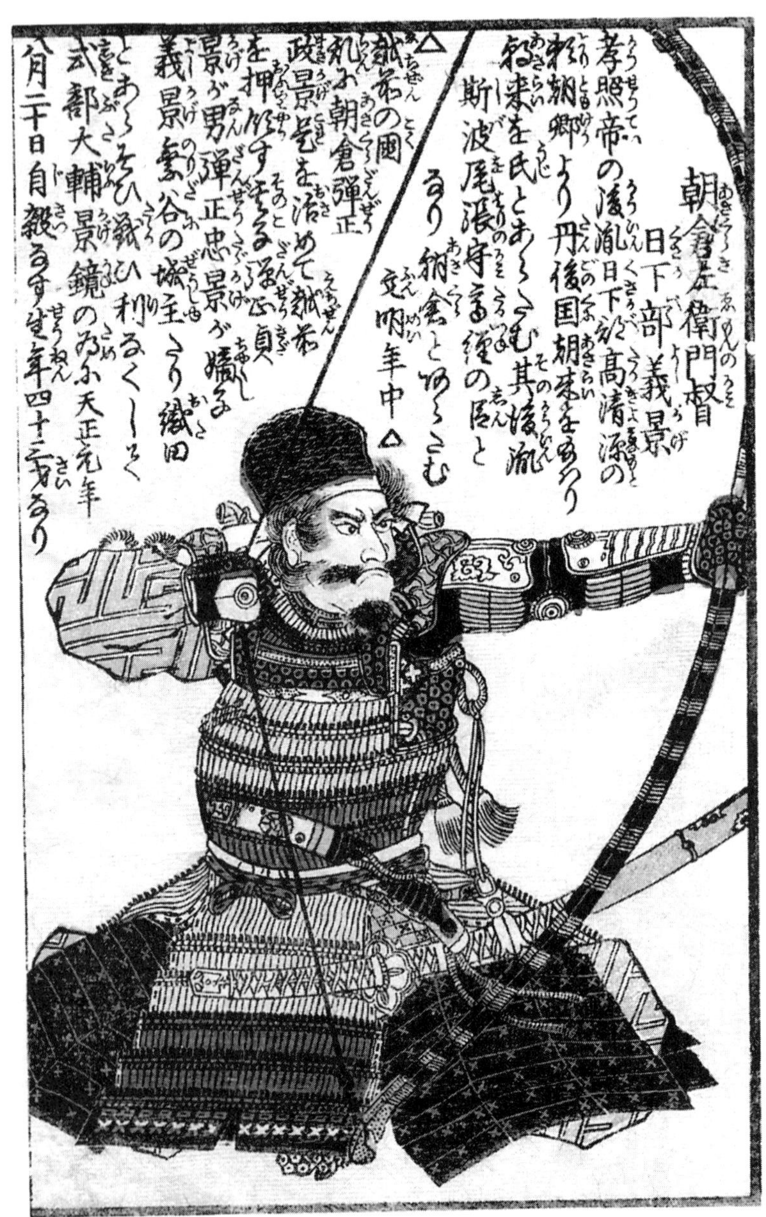

PLATE 28

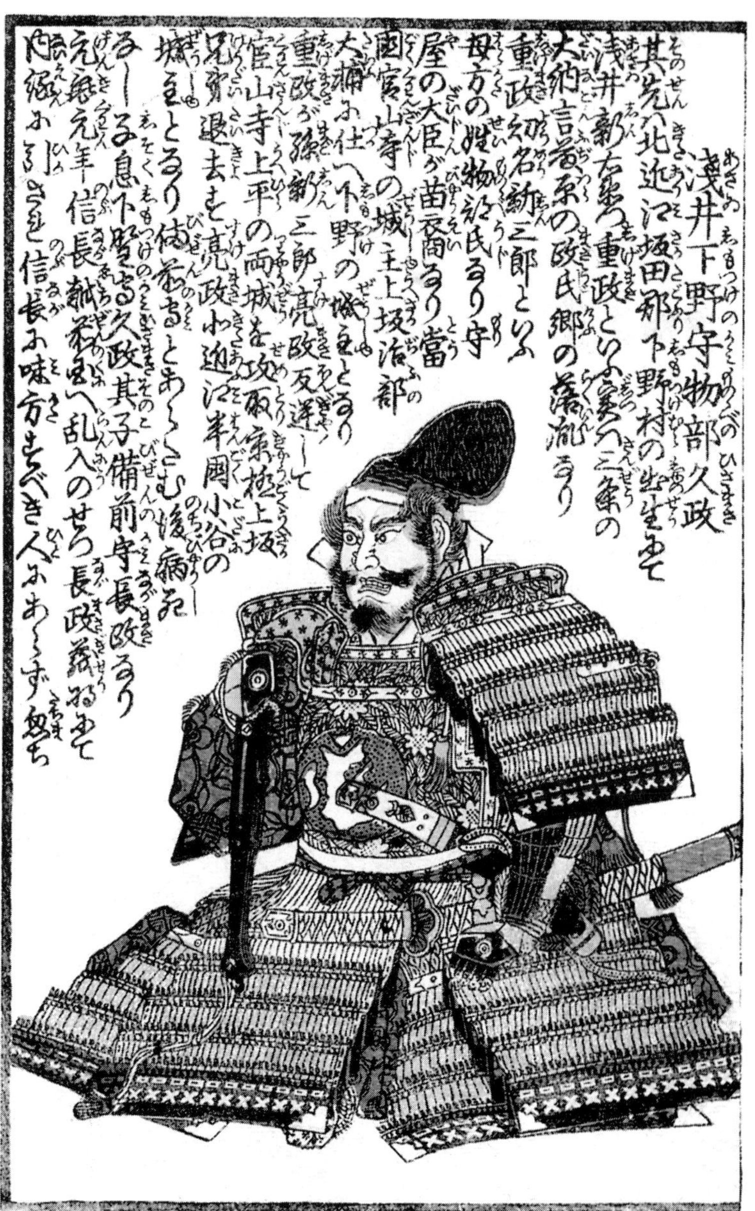

PLATE 29

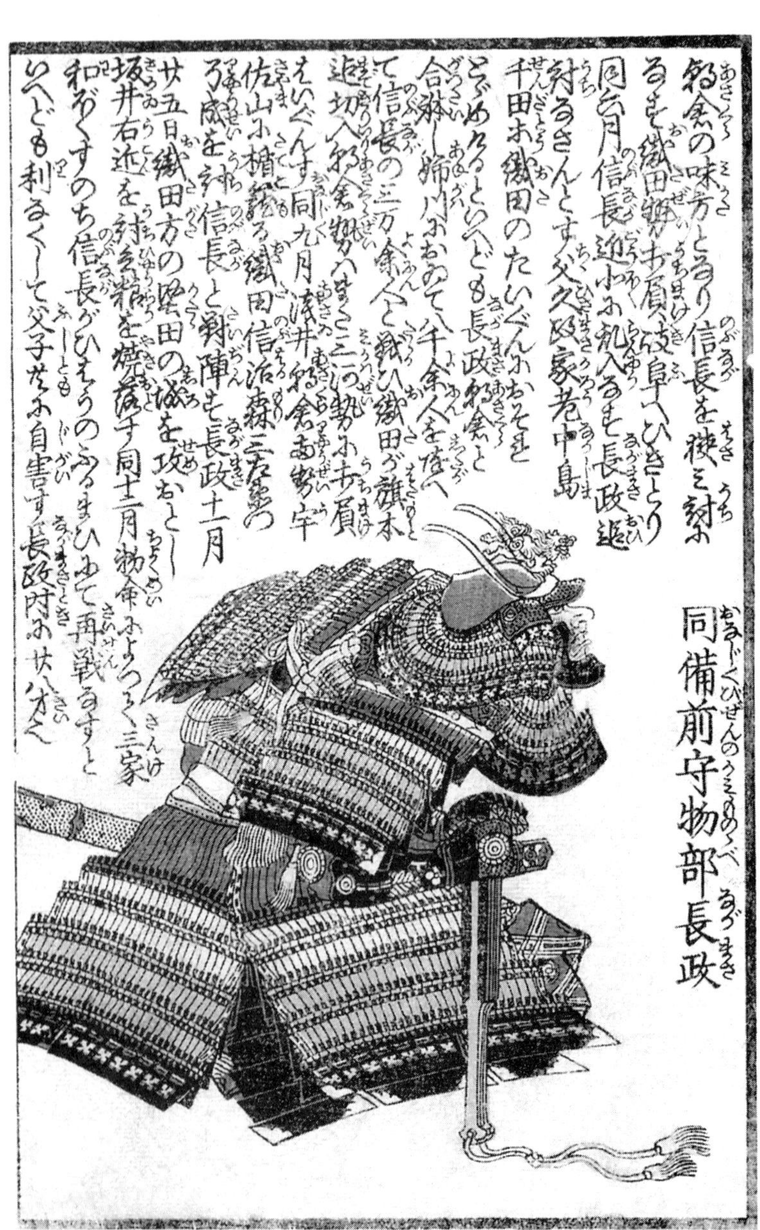

PLATE 30

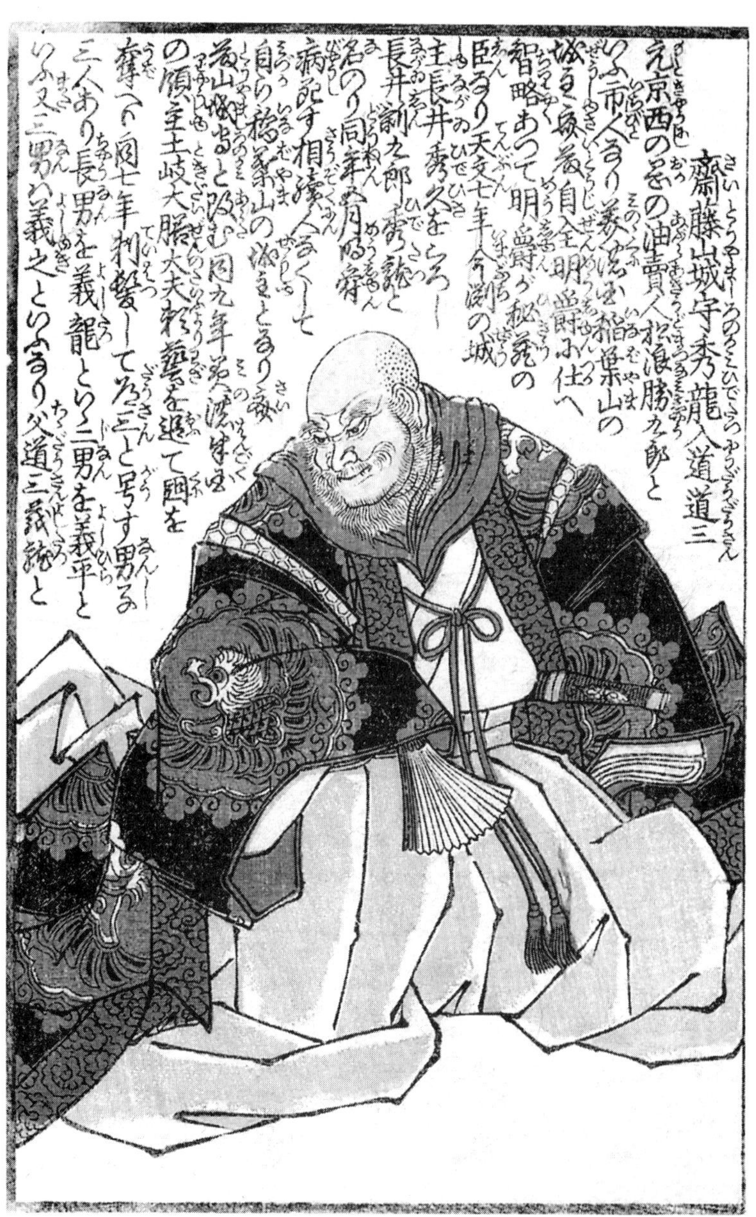

Plate 31

同治部大輔義龍

不和にして二男義平を家督にせんとす義龍是を安からず憤り弘治二年正月道三道野に狩せしひまに両弟を城中にまねき勇士日根野下野守に討とらす道三是を怒り義龍を殺さんと軍勢を集めけると雖義龍七千余人引率して道三が居城稲葉山を攻ける道三運尽て討死なす時に年齢六十三才なり義龍自立して稲葉山に在城す永禄四年七月熱病を煩ひて是に死す嫡子龍興へ美濃の國を治むるといへども普代の老臣の云事をもちひずしてつねに敵のためにそしられ當家第一の三老臣稲葉安藤氏江ゐるとりに織田家へ降参す竹中半兵衛ハ故ありてさき山林に隠退す永禄四年五月信長志のびて上洛せしときは勢三十人ばかり引ぐしのびて信長を討んと

つぎへ

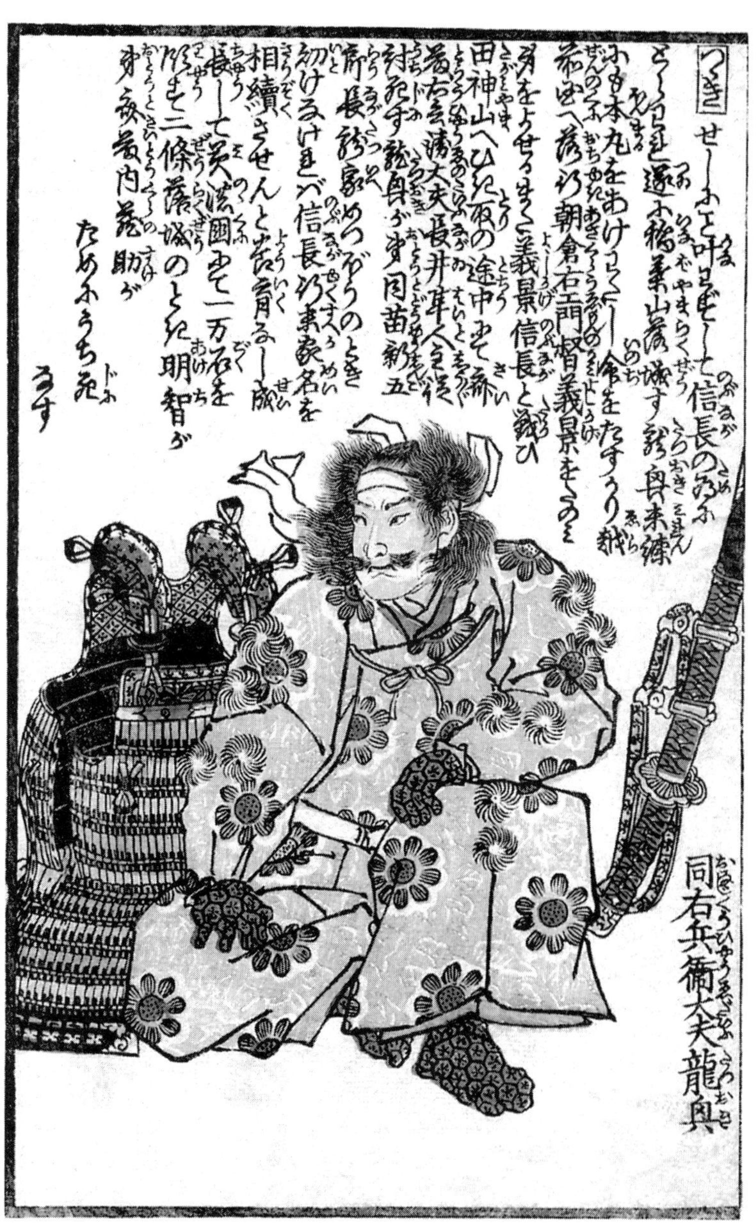

PLATE 33

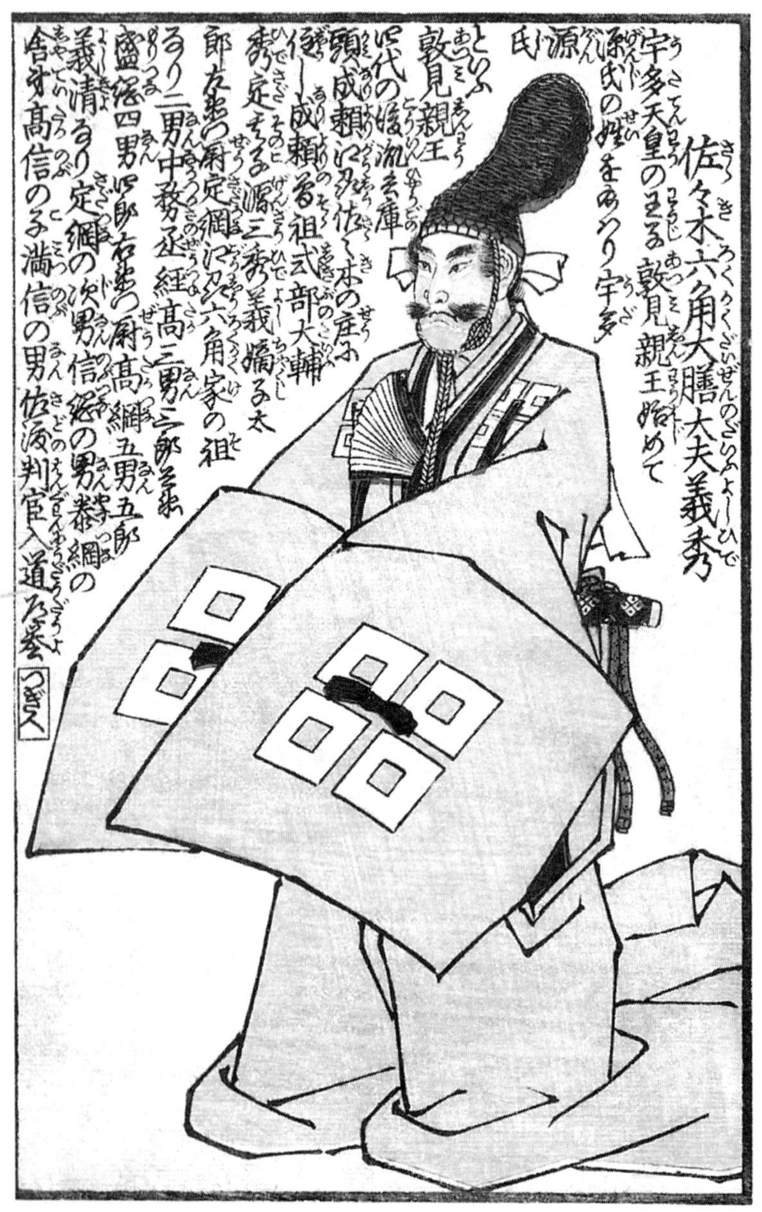

Plate 34

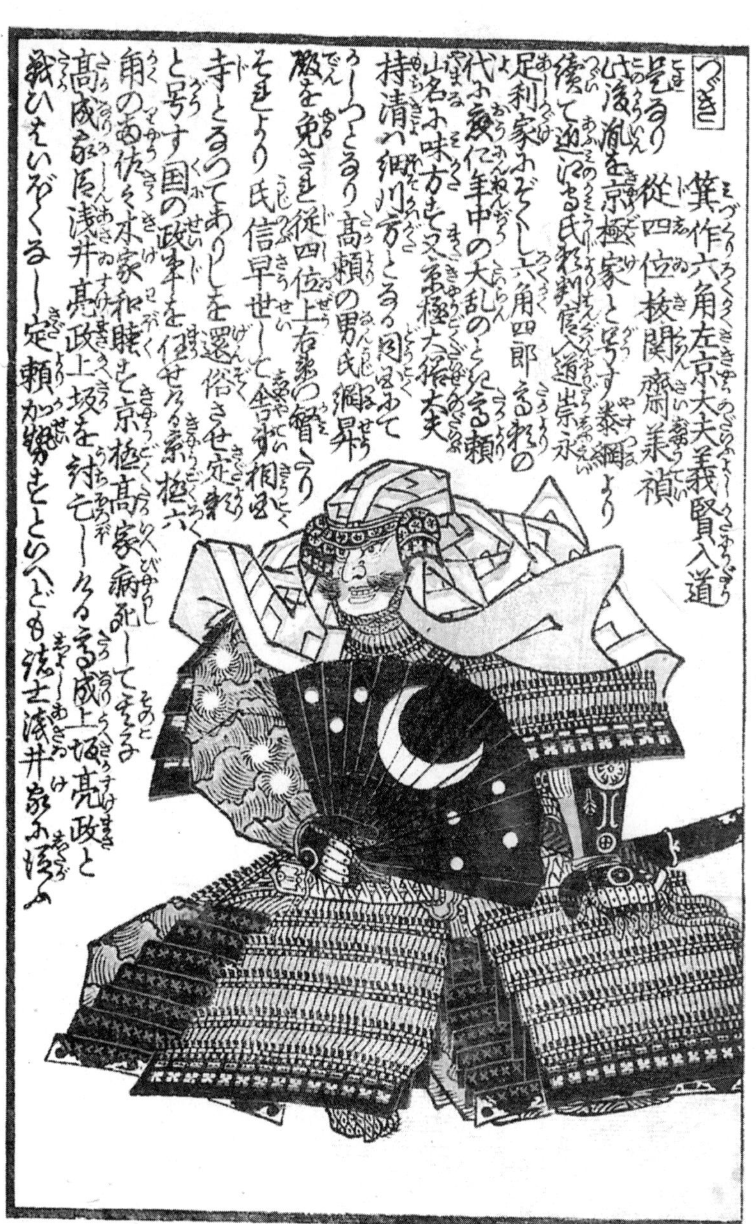

Plate 35

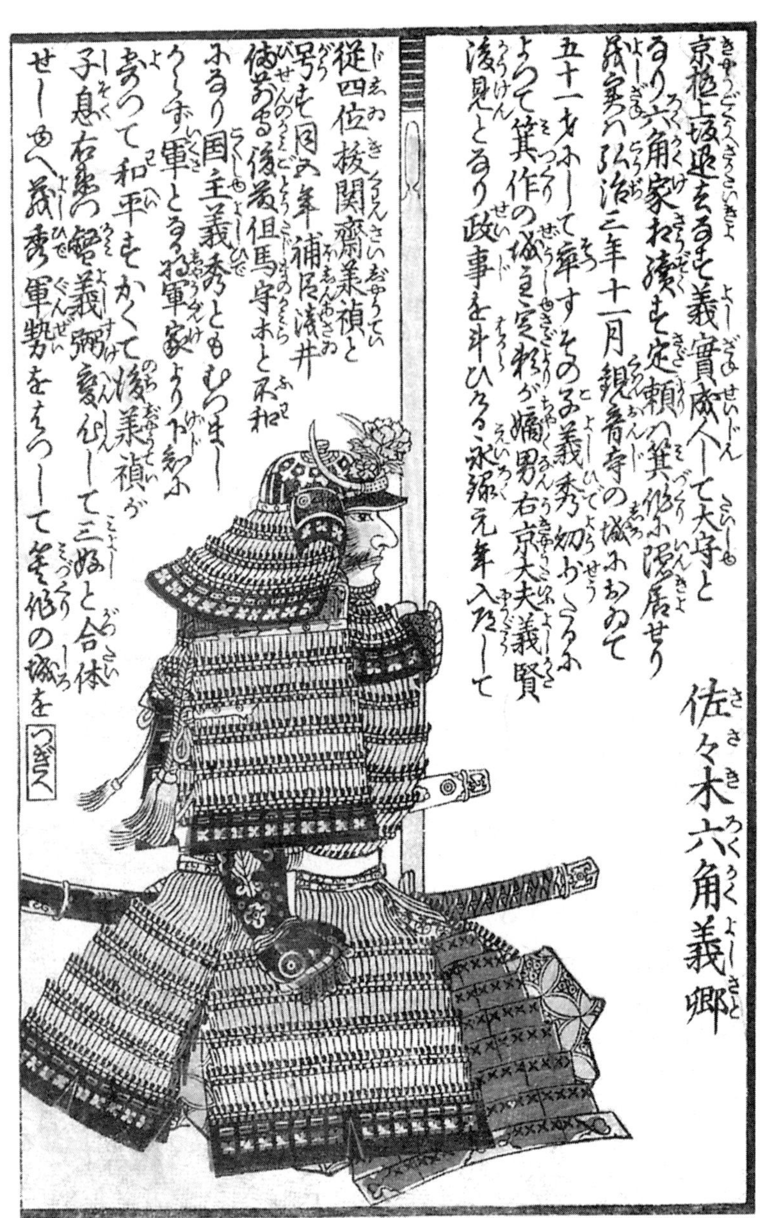

PLATE 36

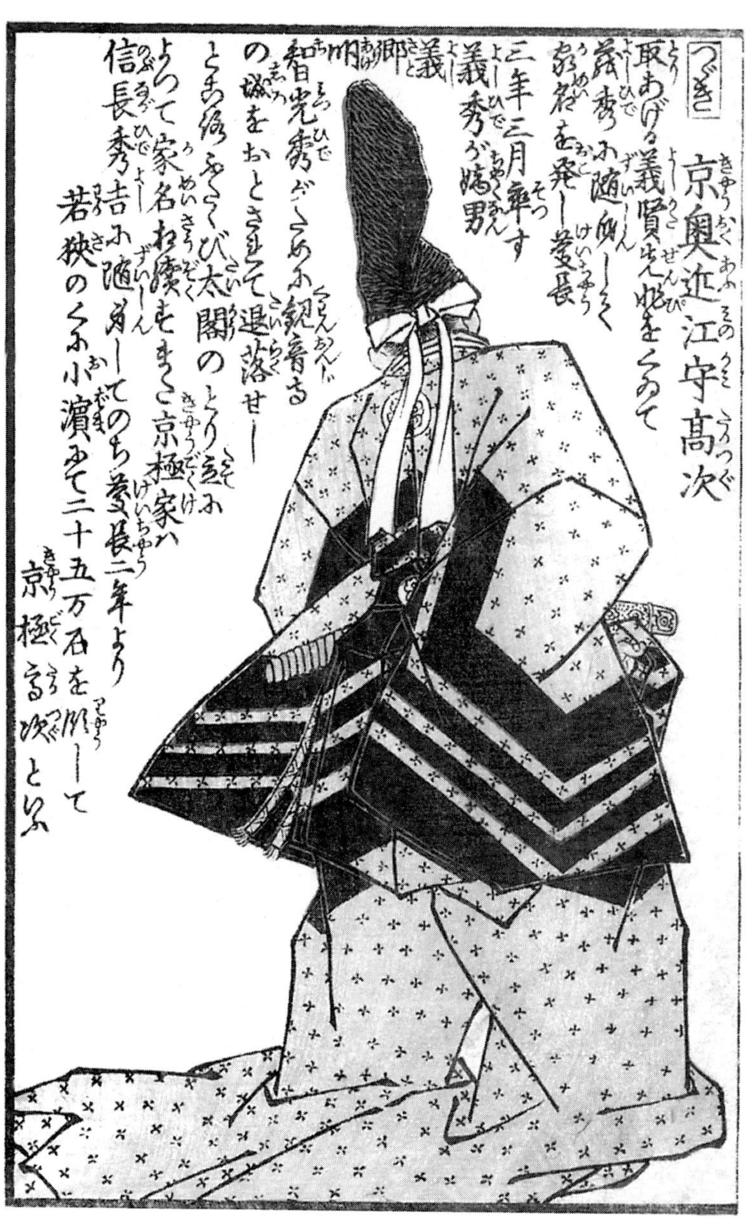

京奥近江守高次

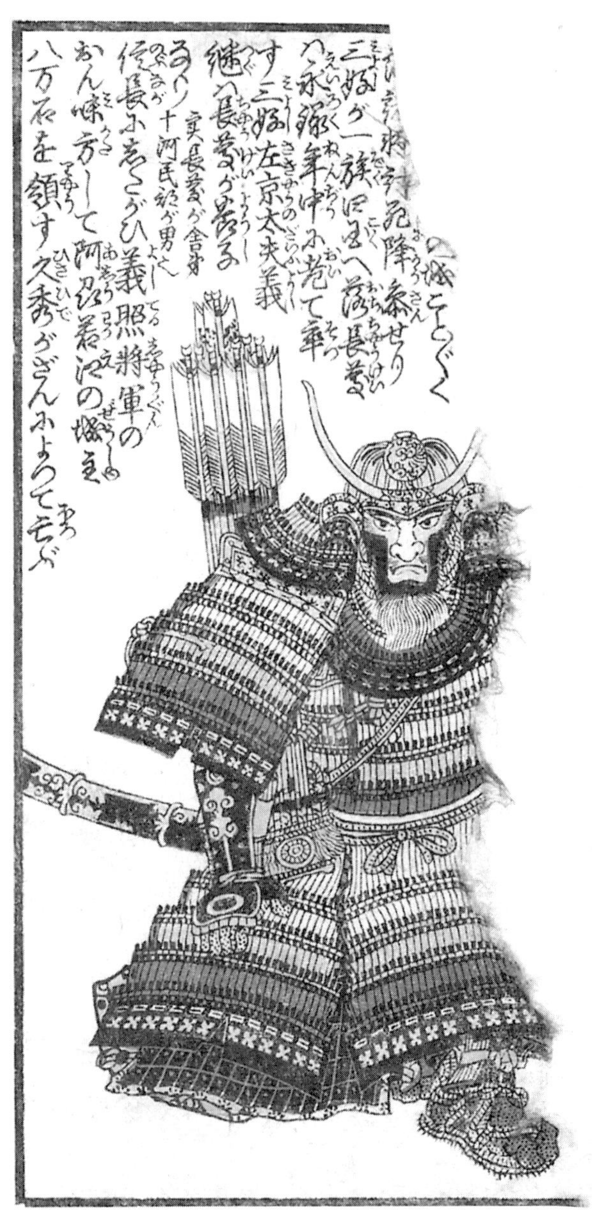

Plate 38

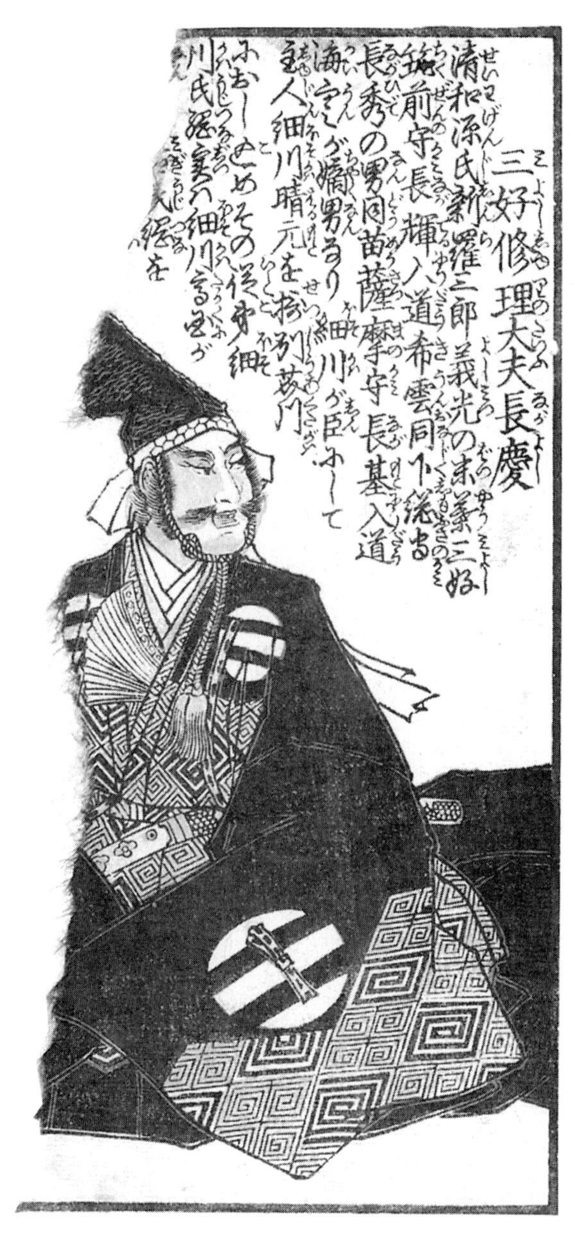

Plate 39

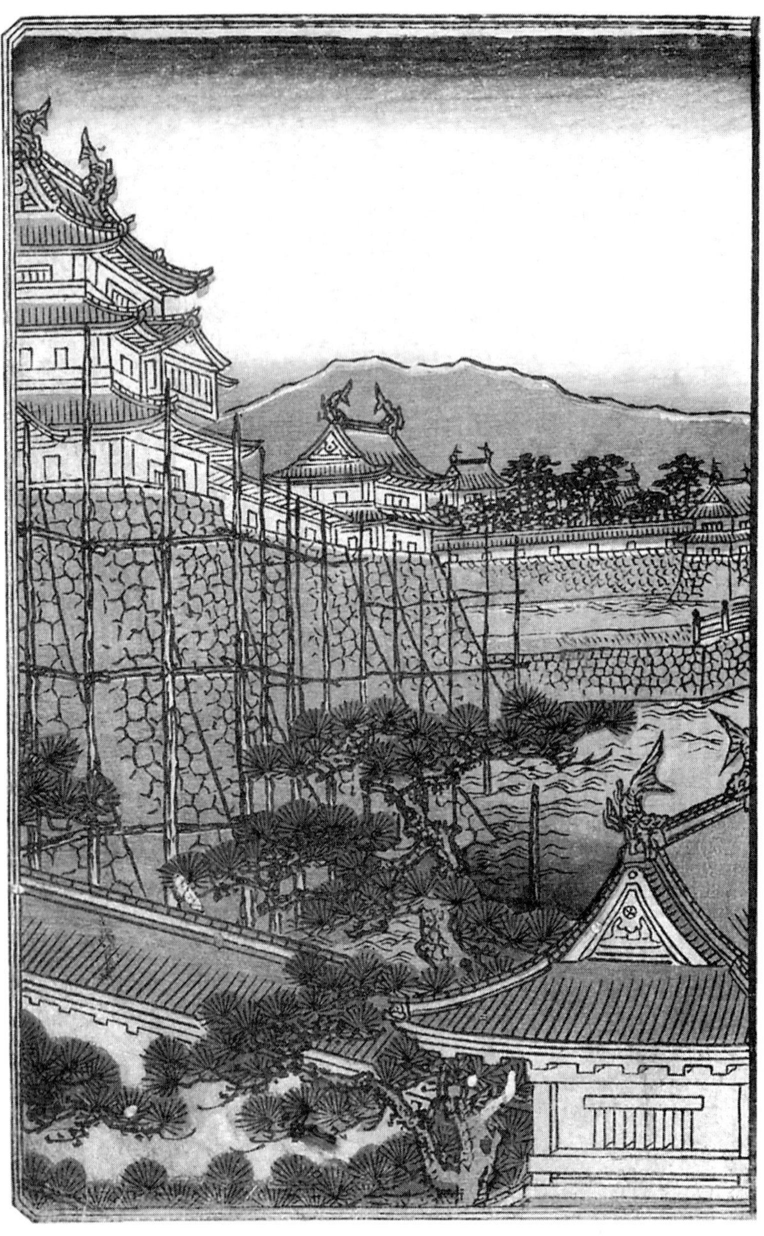

Plate 40

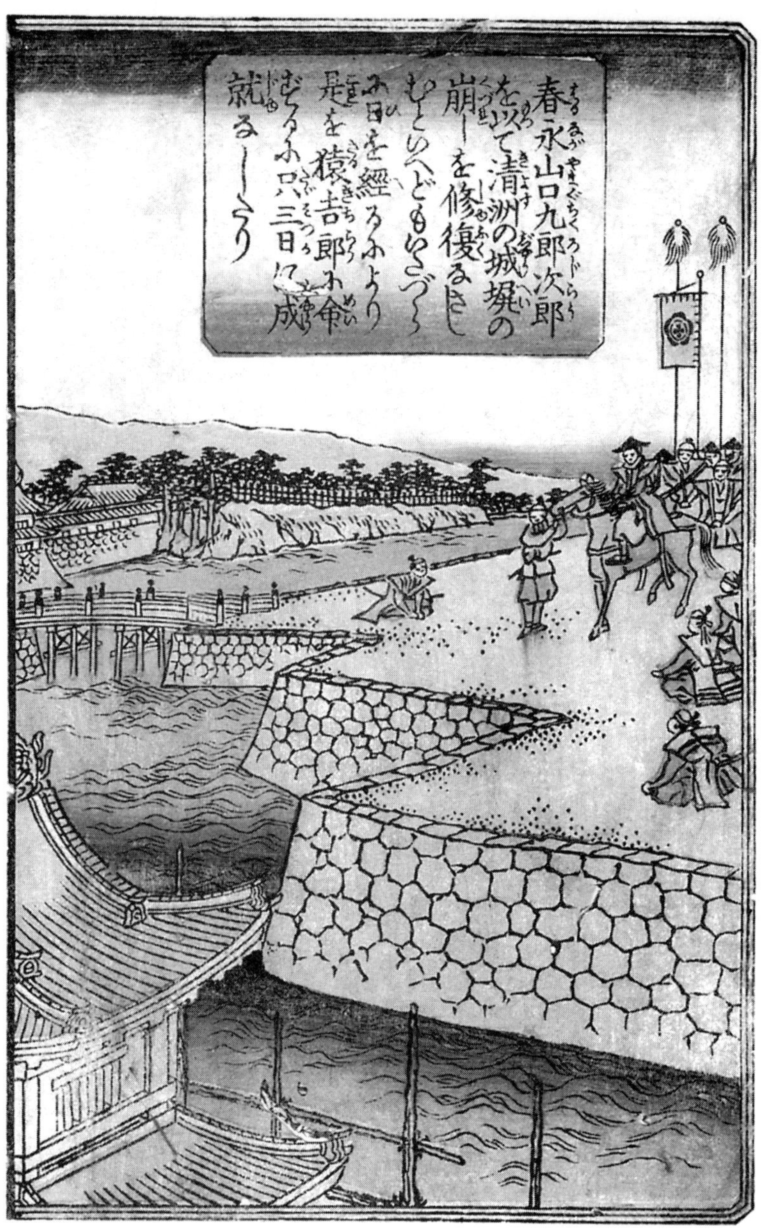
春永山口九郎次郎
を以て清洲の城塀の
崩しを修復さし
むといへどもはかどらず
多日を經るにより
是を猿吉郎に命
ぜらるゝに只三日に成
就なしけり

PLATE 41

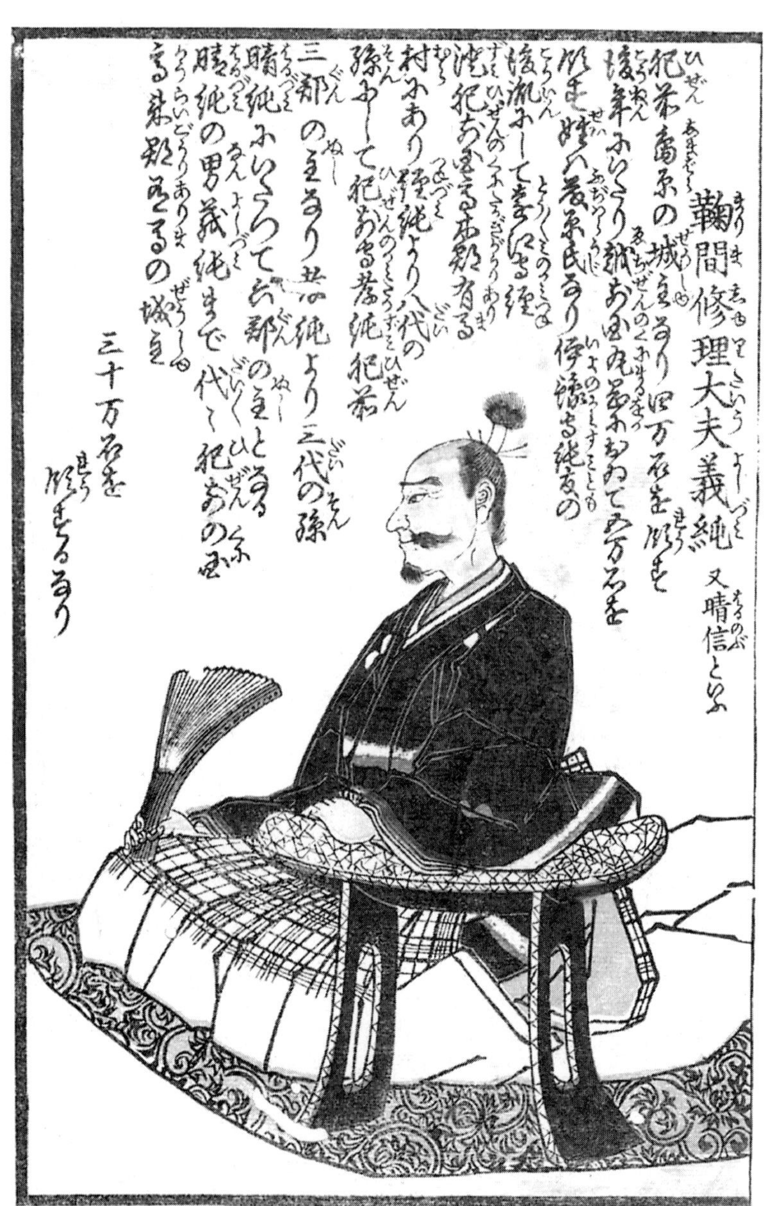

PLATE 42

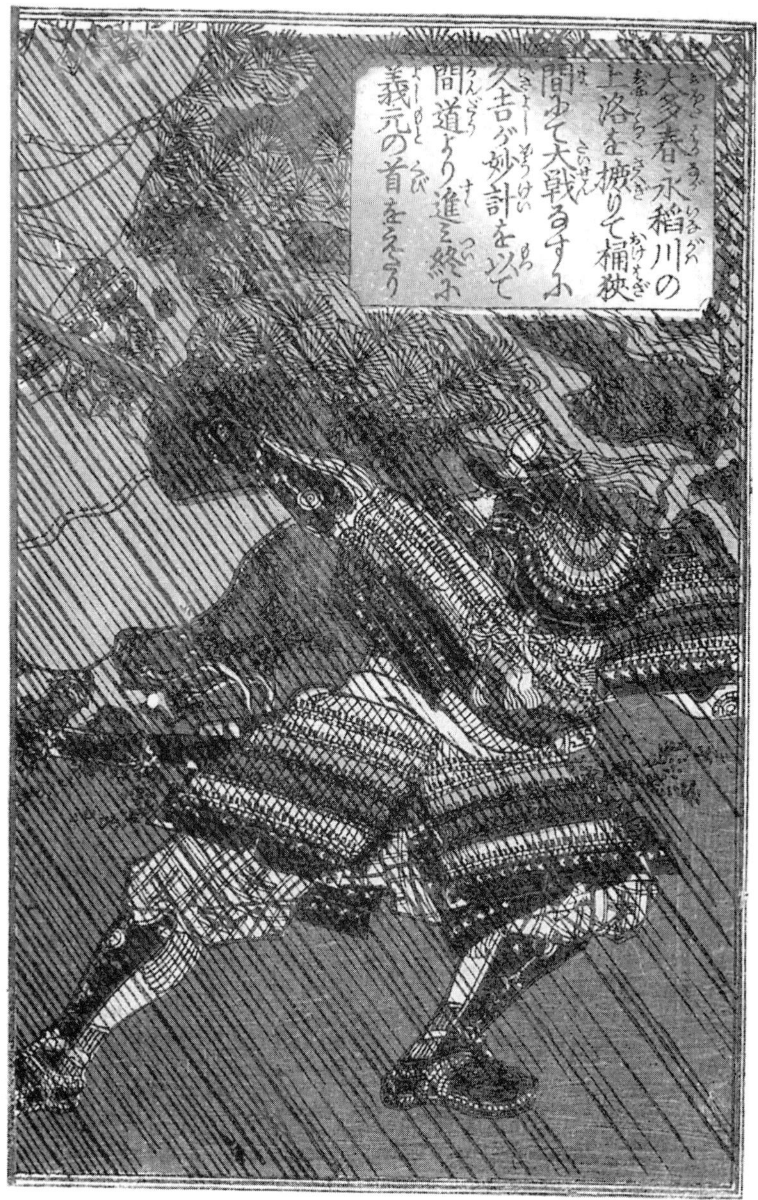

PLATE 43

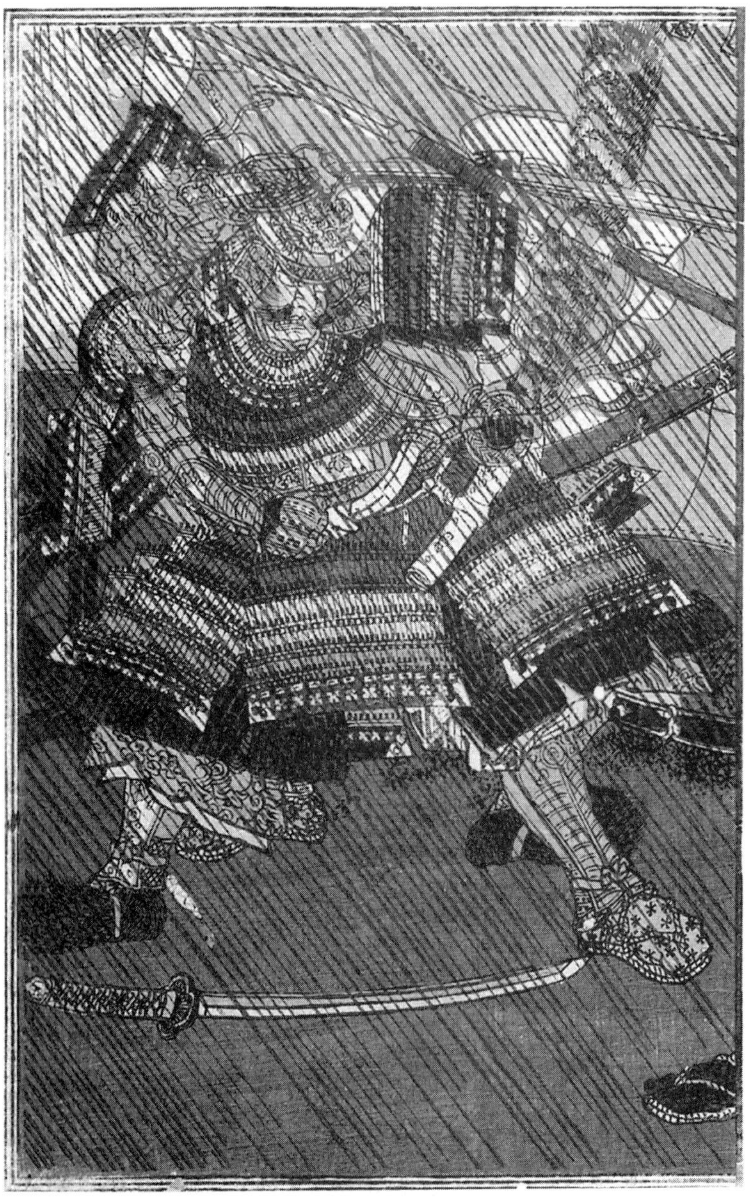

Plate 44

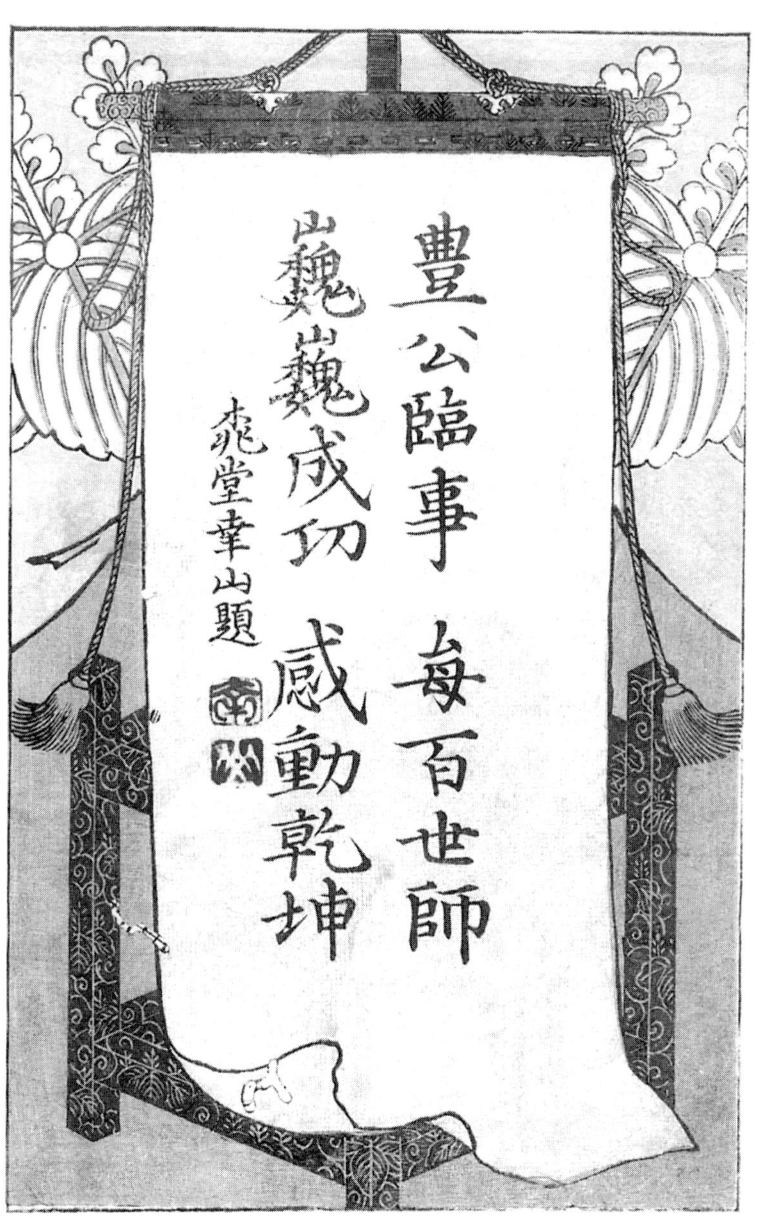

PLATE 45

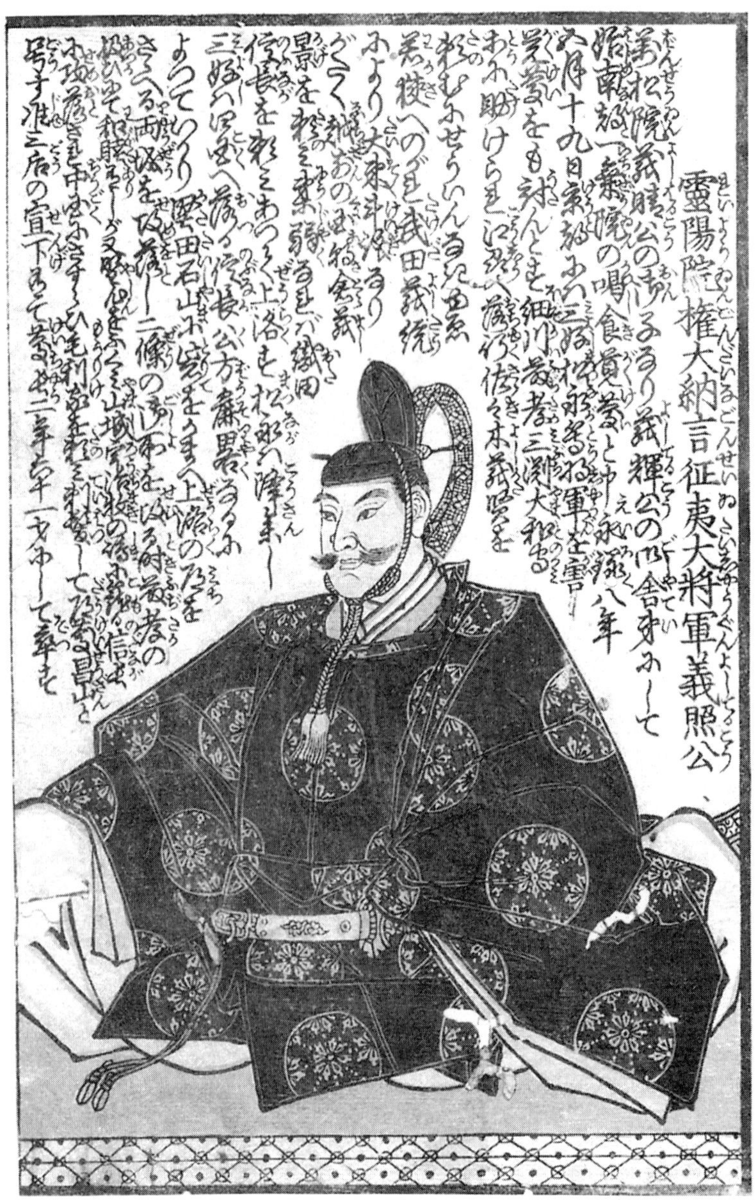

PLATE 46

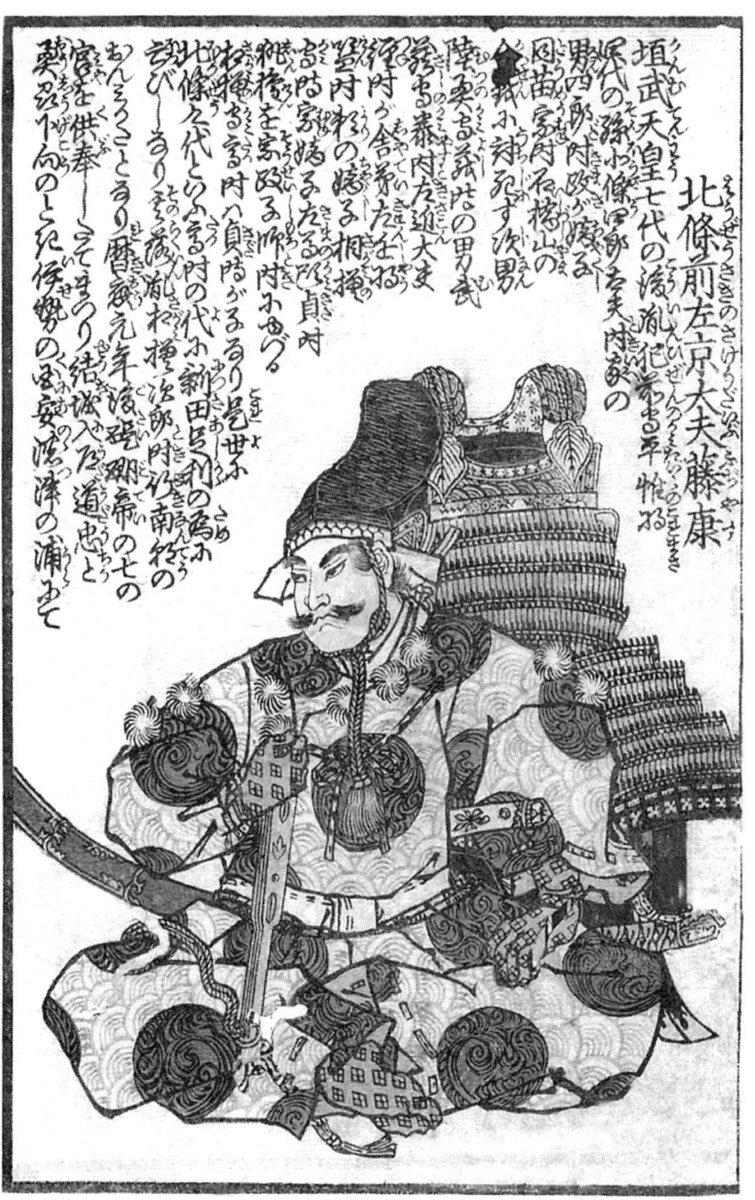

PLATE 47

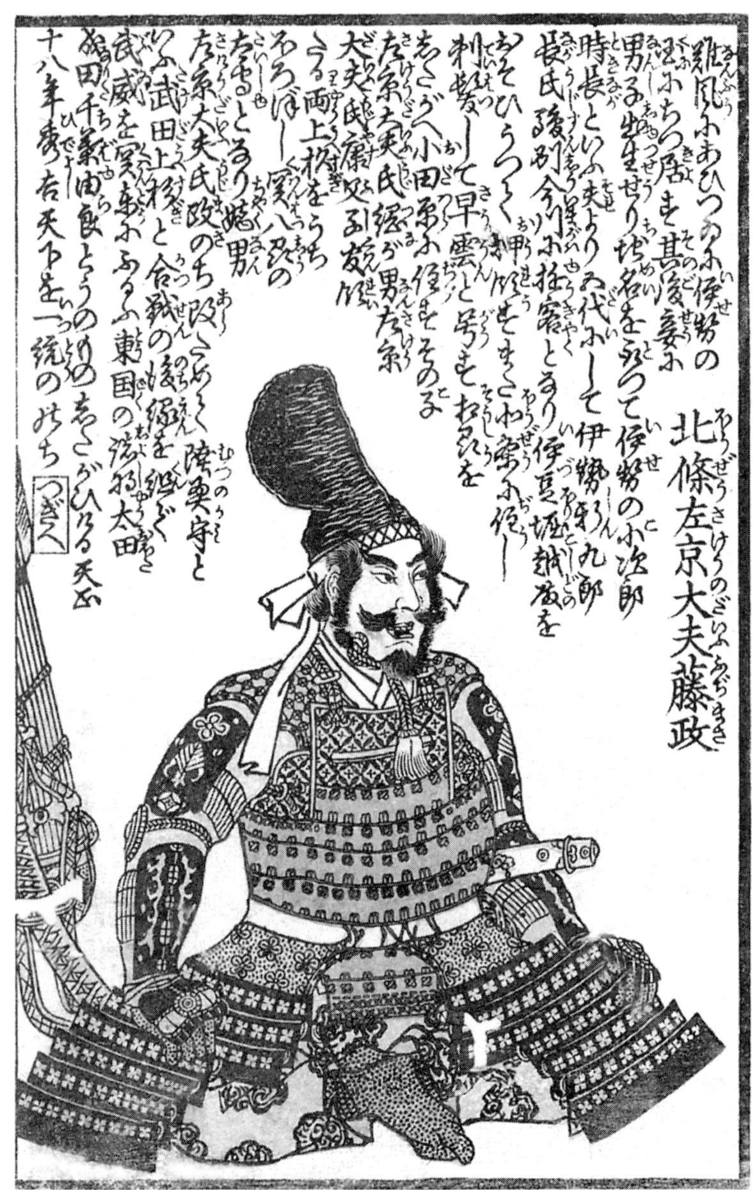

PLATE 48

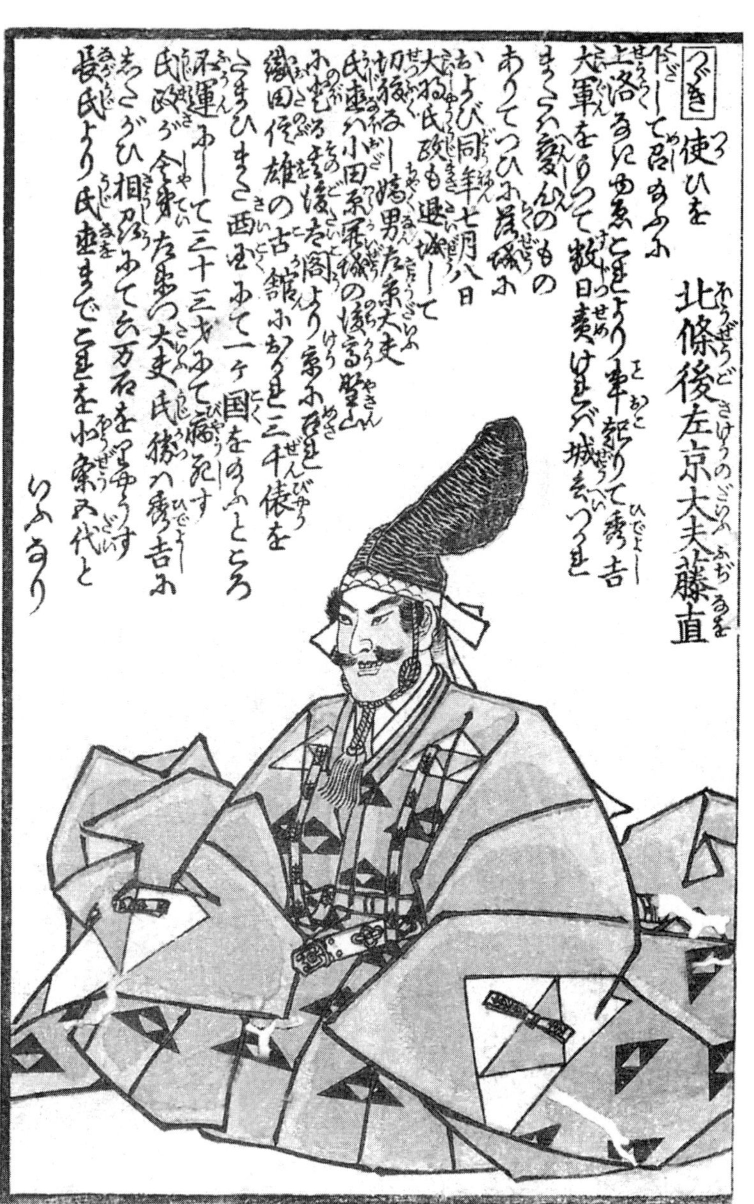

PLATE 49

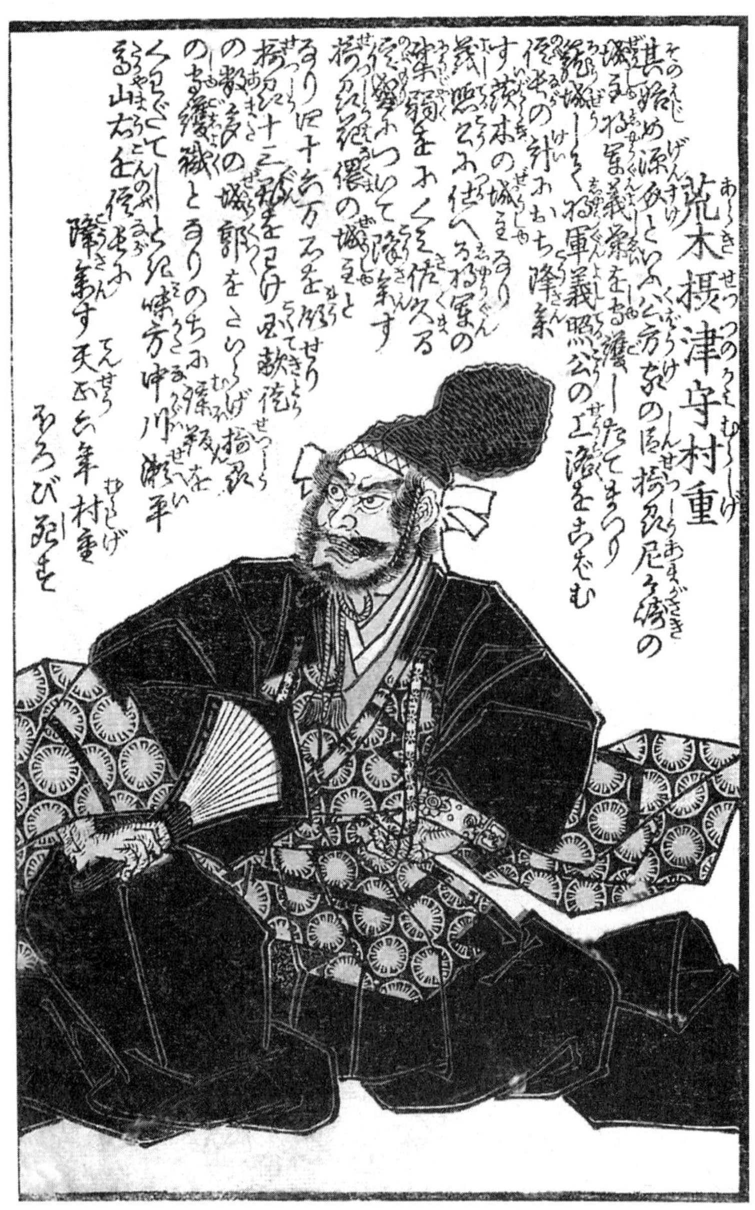

Plate 50

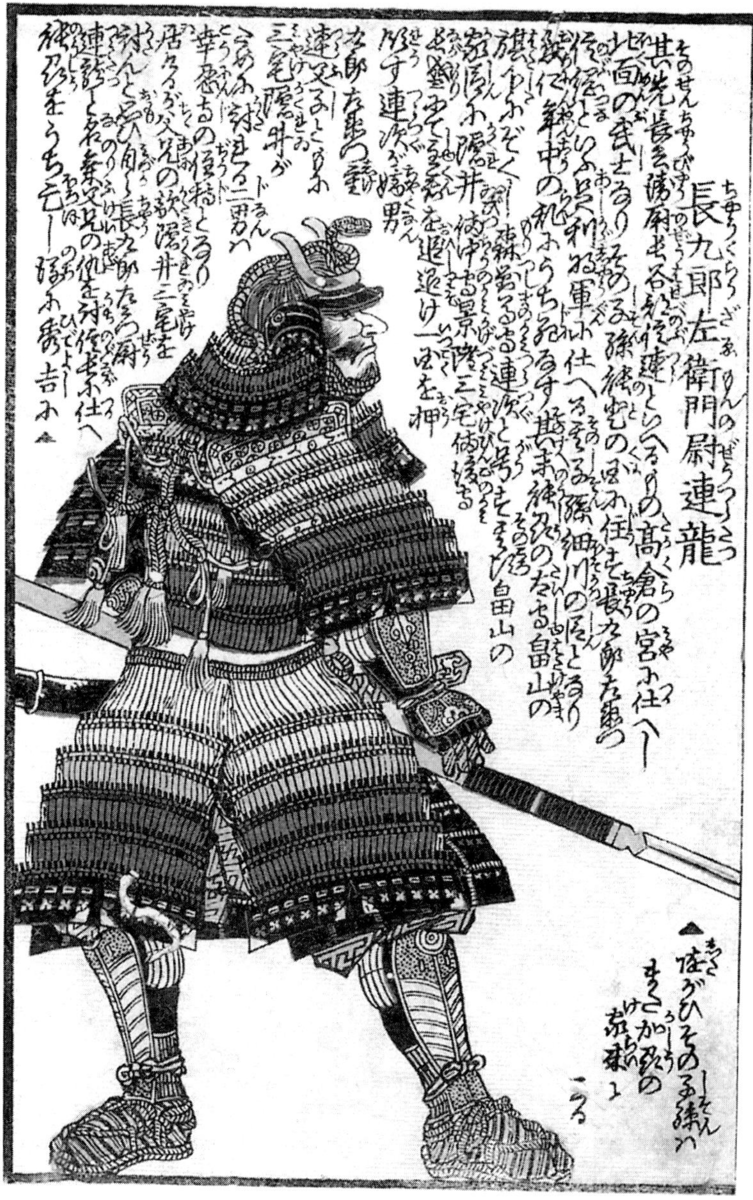

PLATE 51

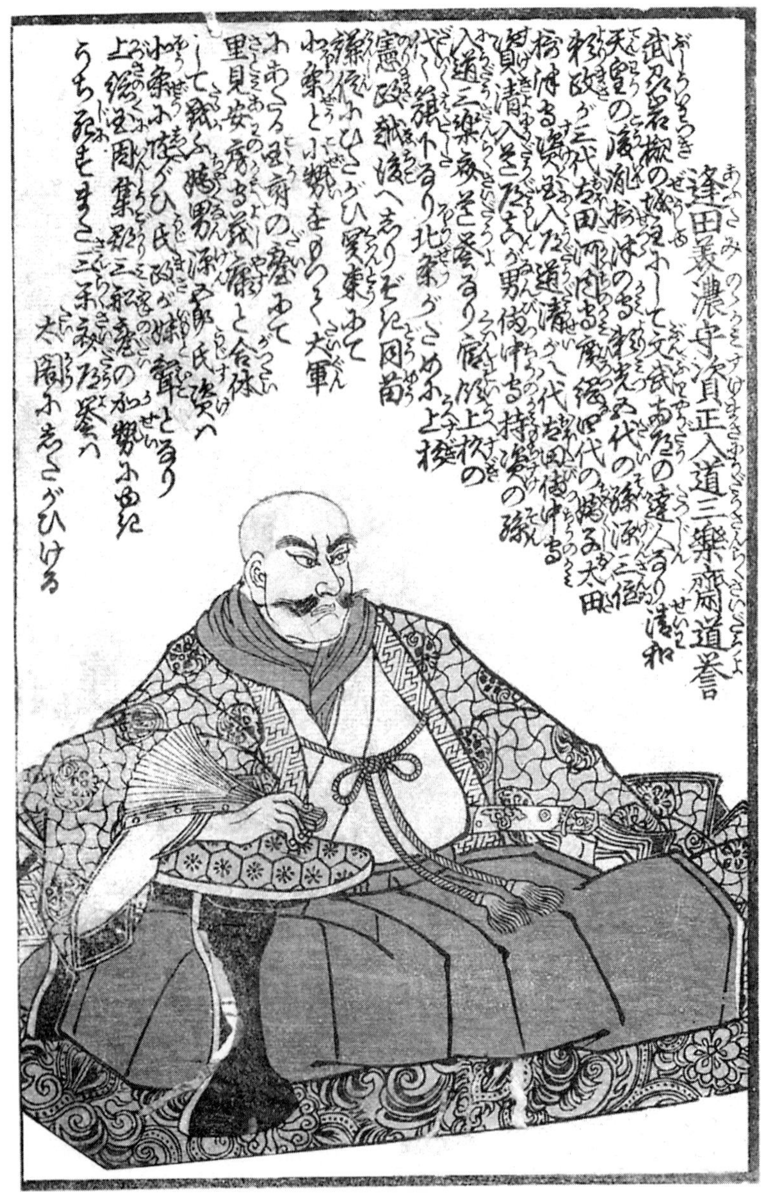

Plate 52

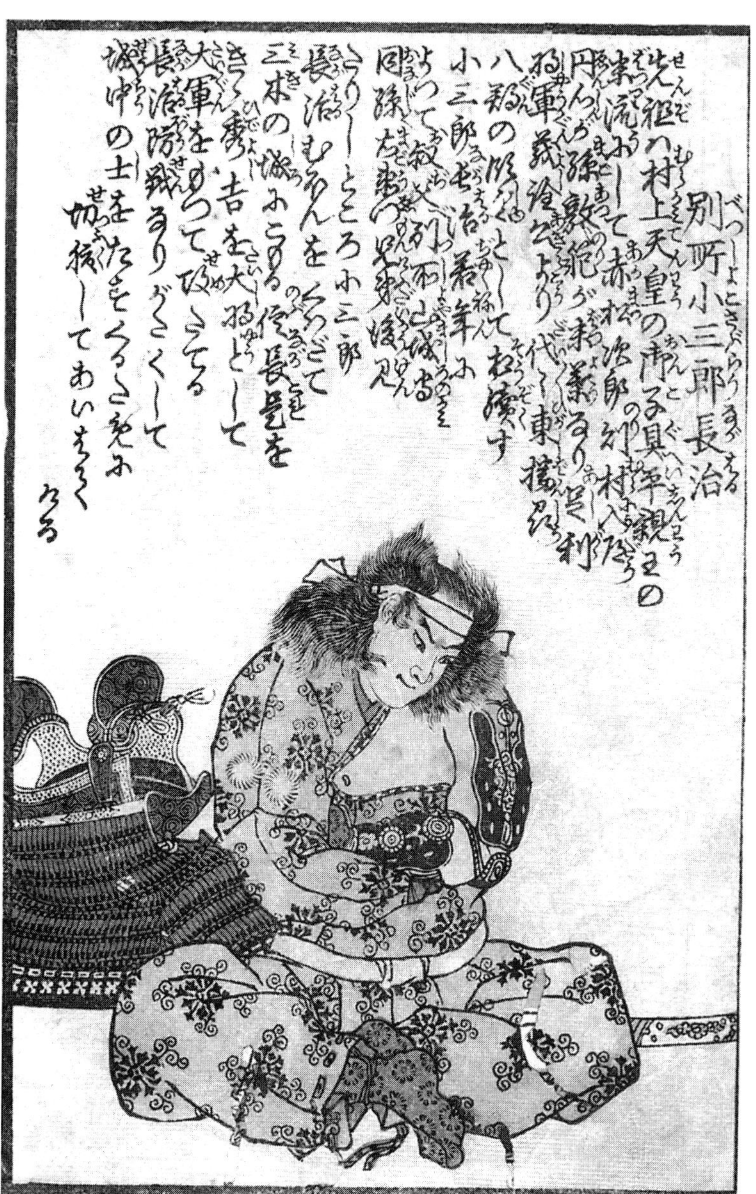

PLATE 53

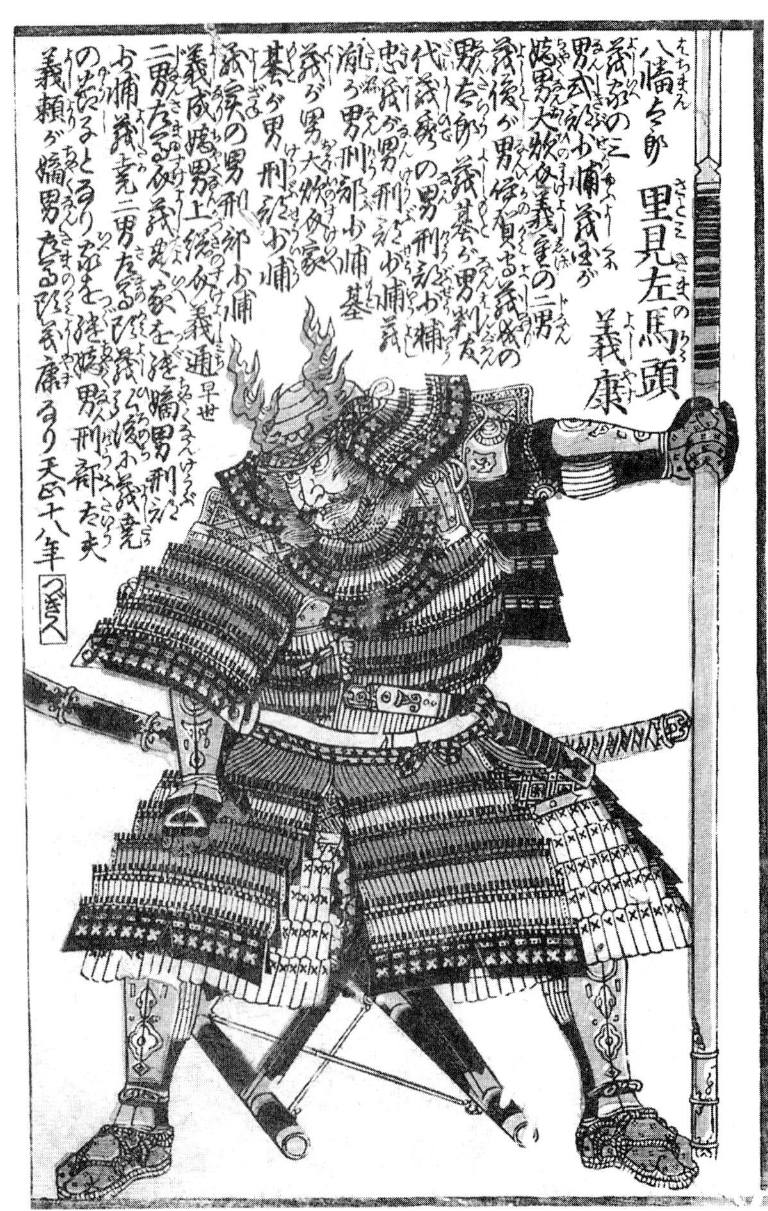

PLATE 54

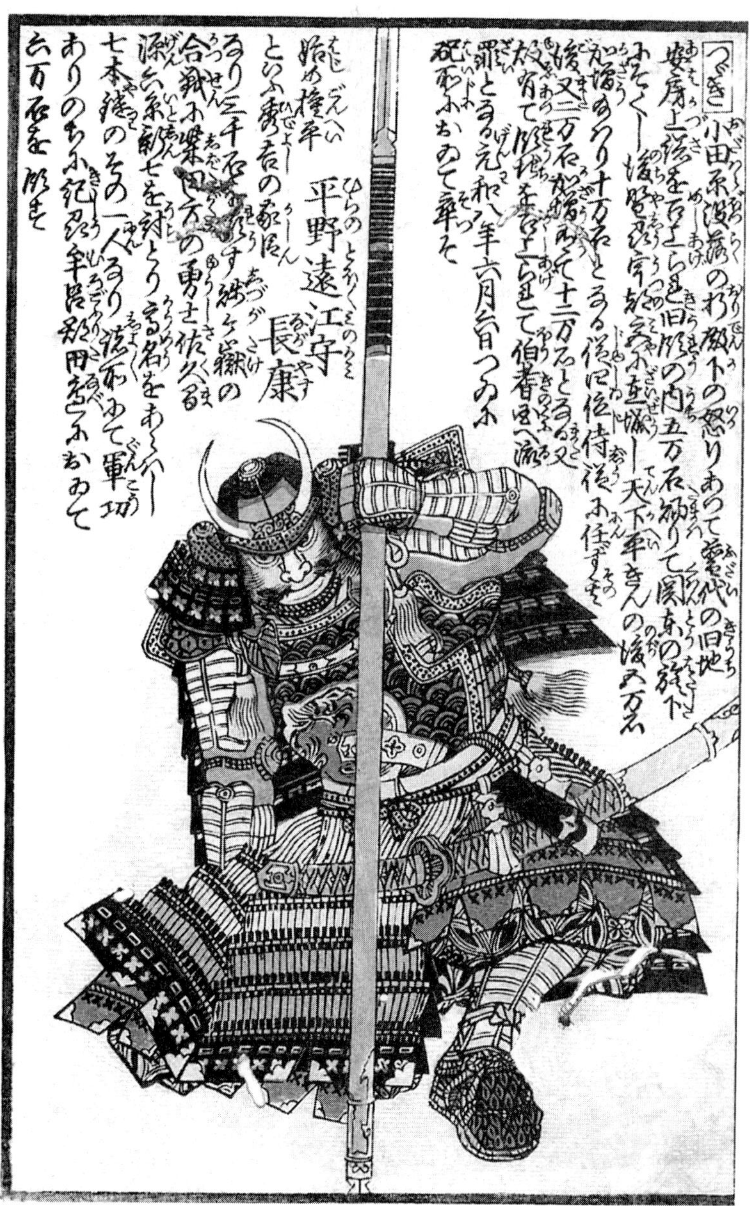

PLATE 55

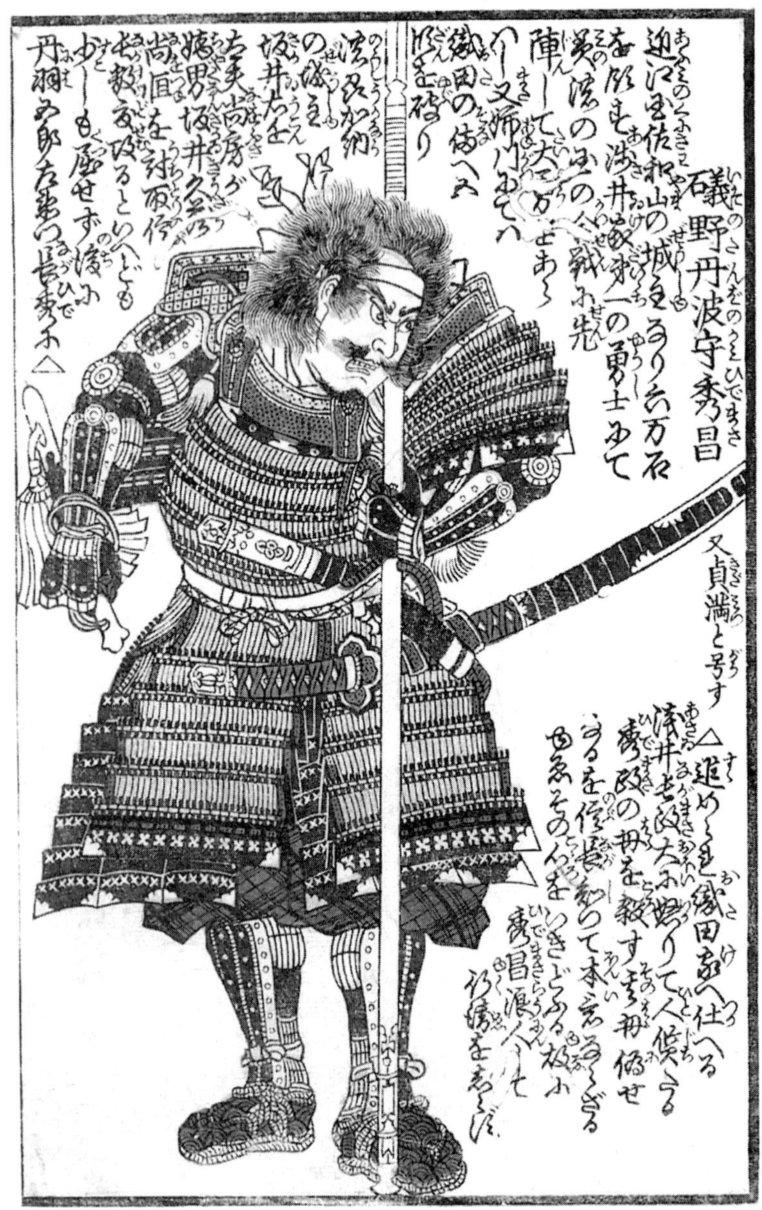

Plate 56

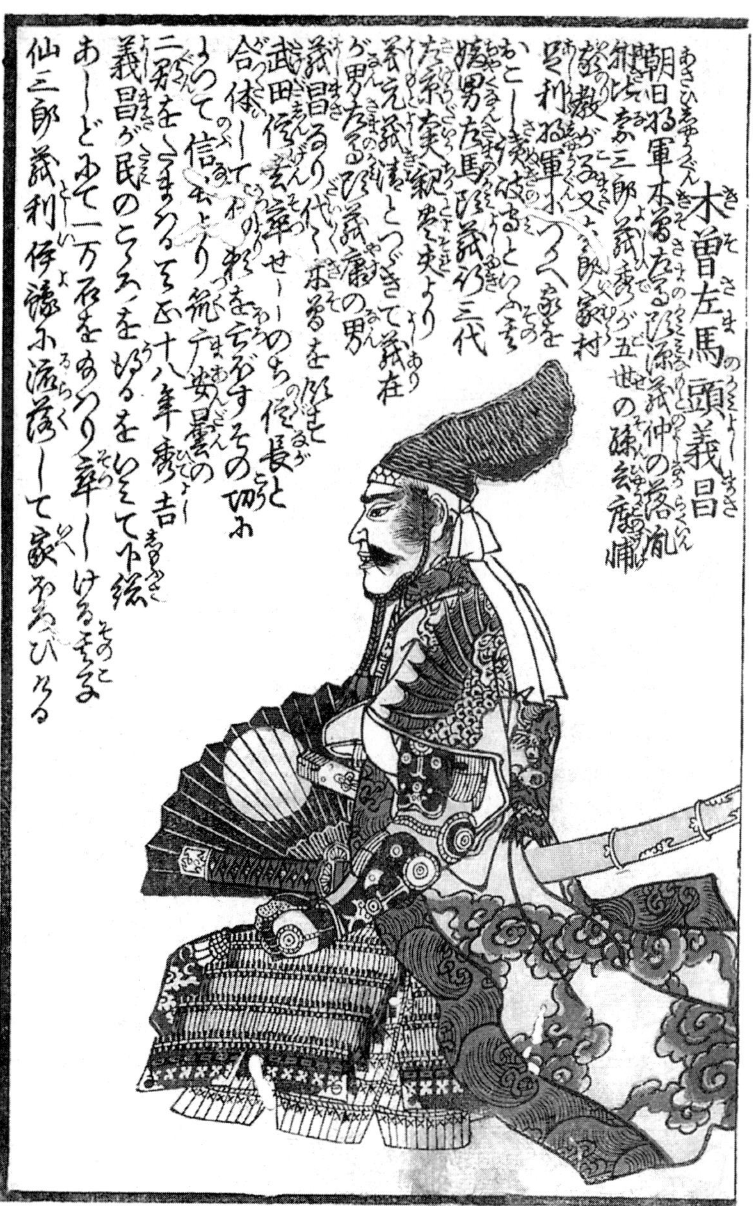

Plate 57

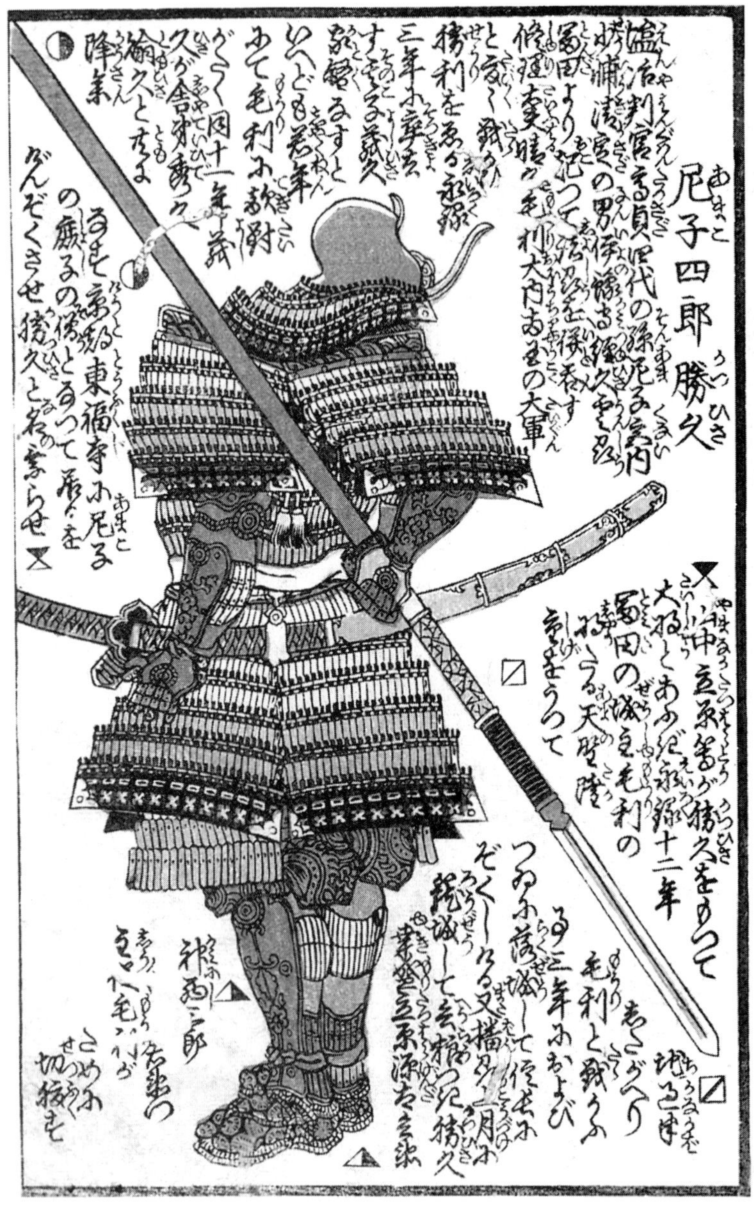

PLATE 58

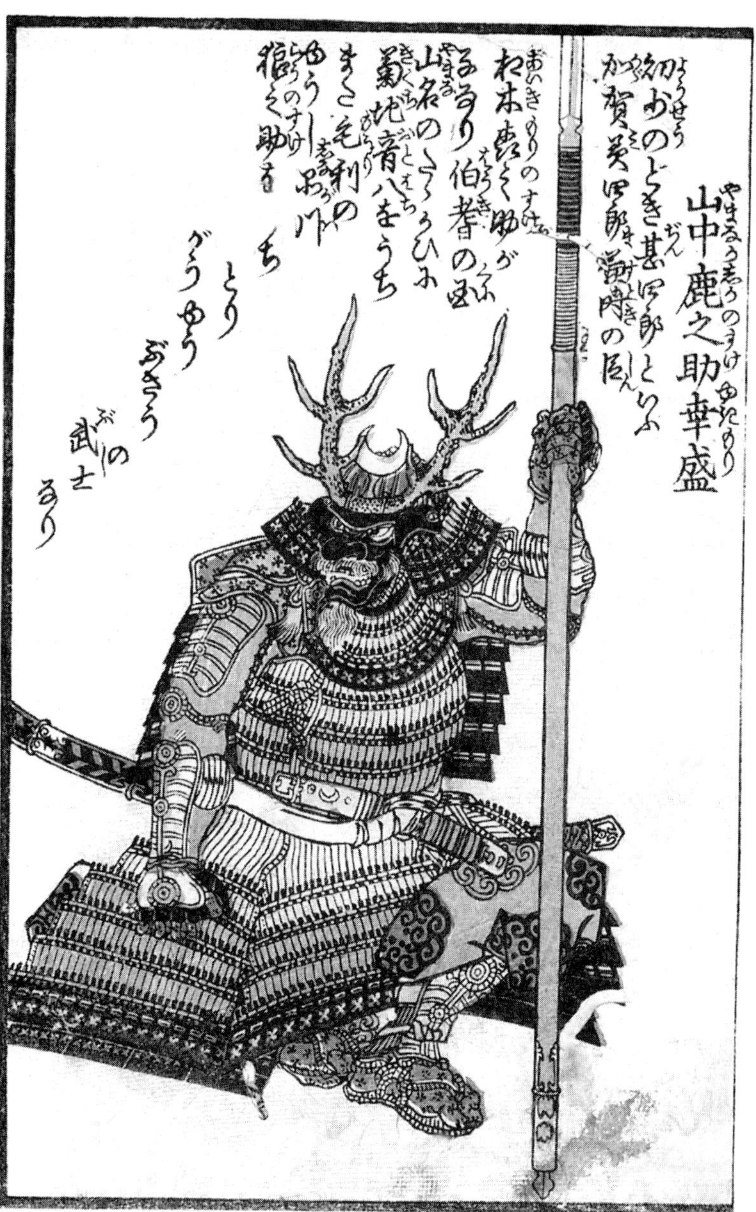

PLATE 59

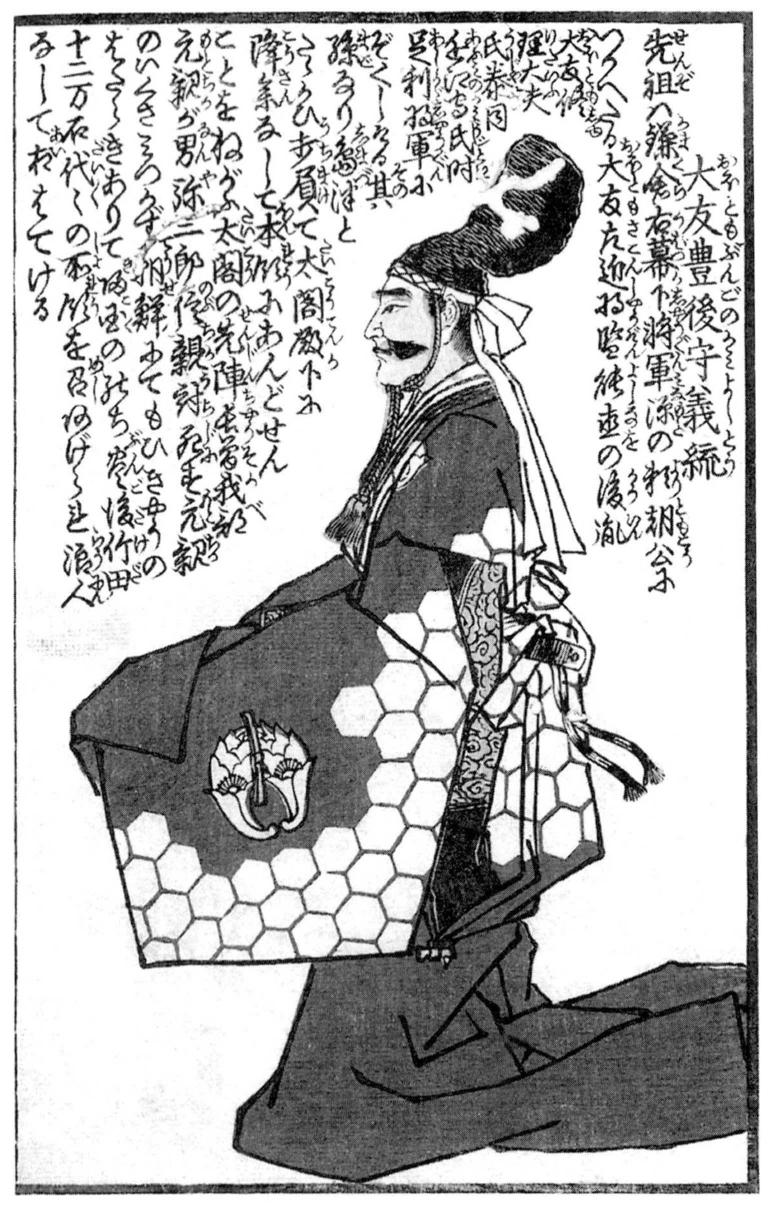

Plate 60

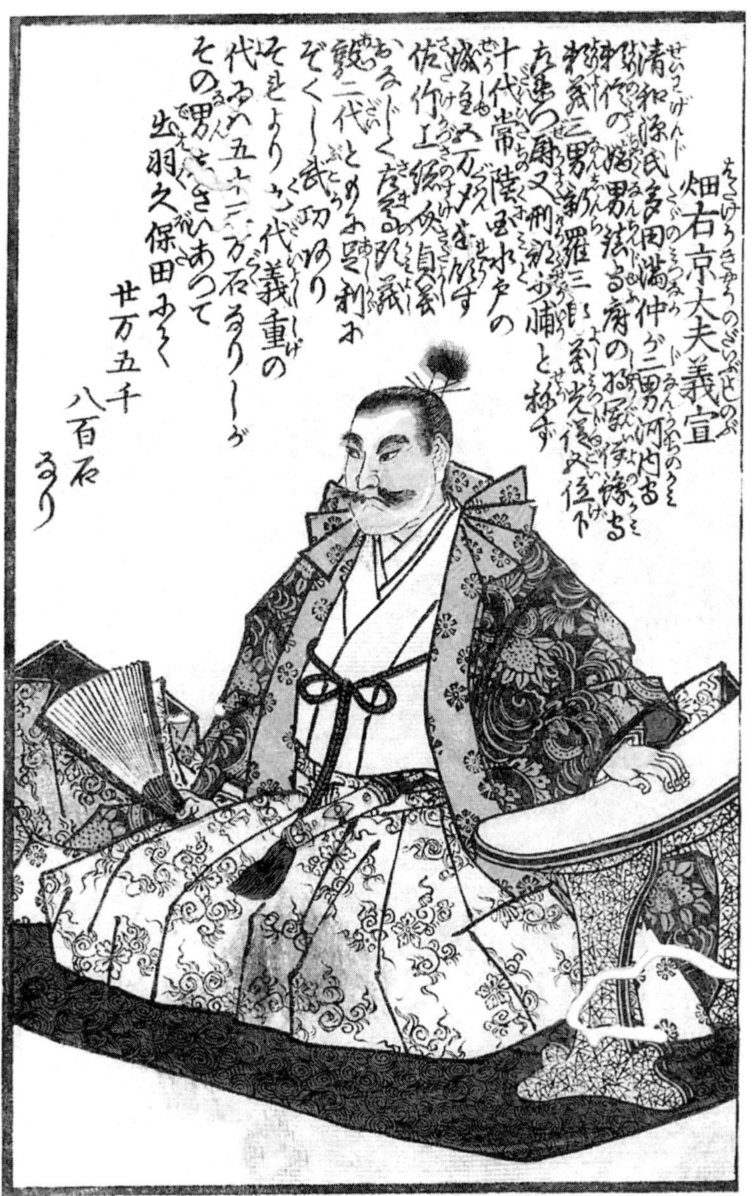

PLATE 61

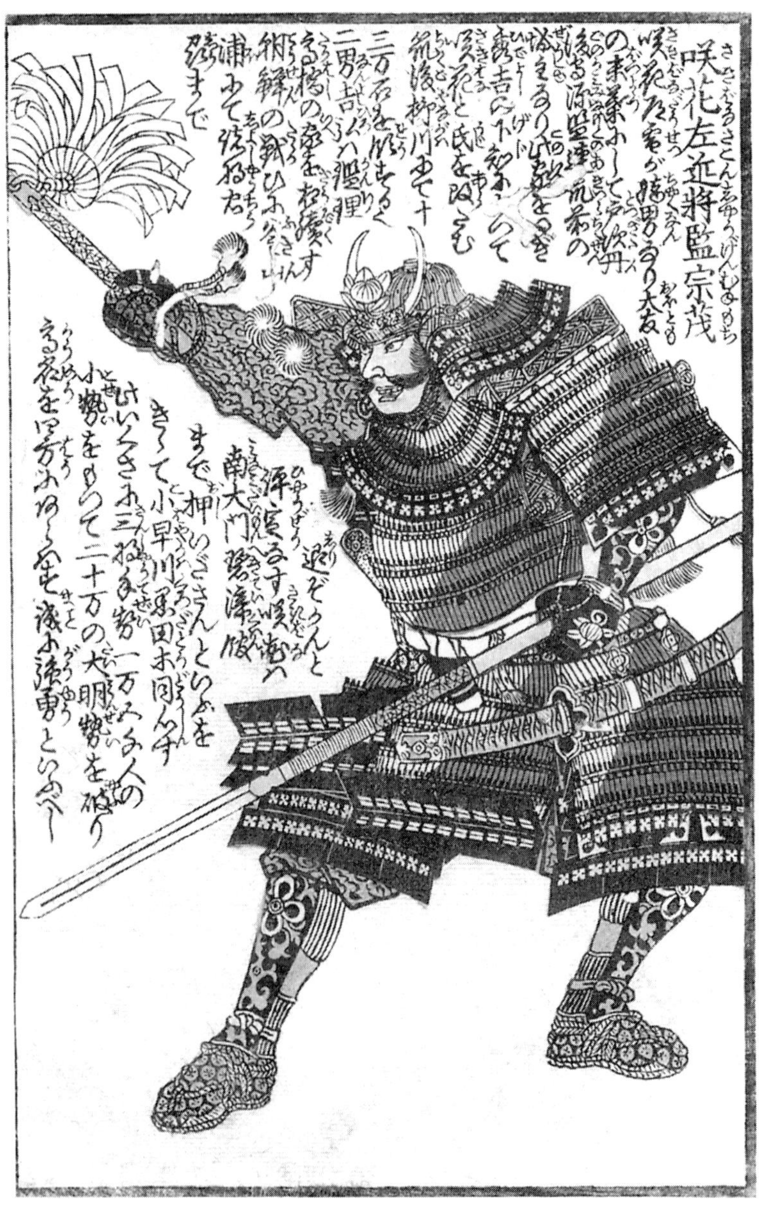

PLATE 62

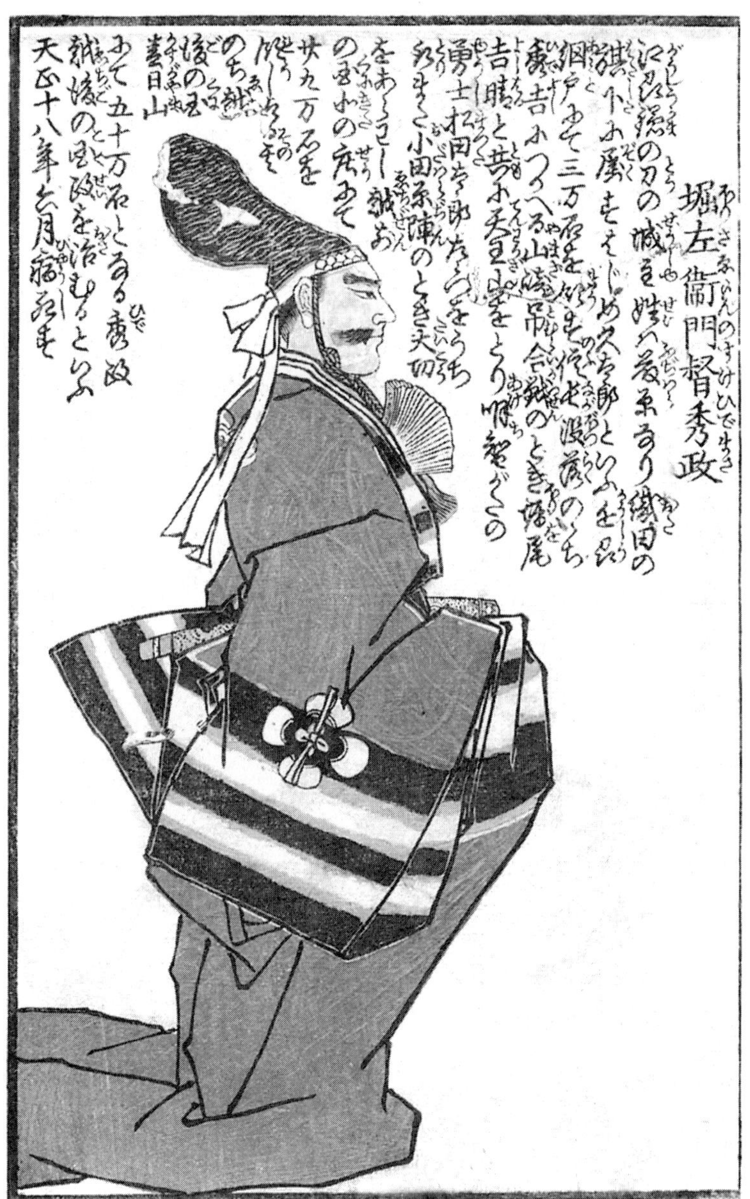

PLATE 63

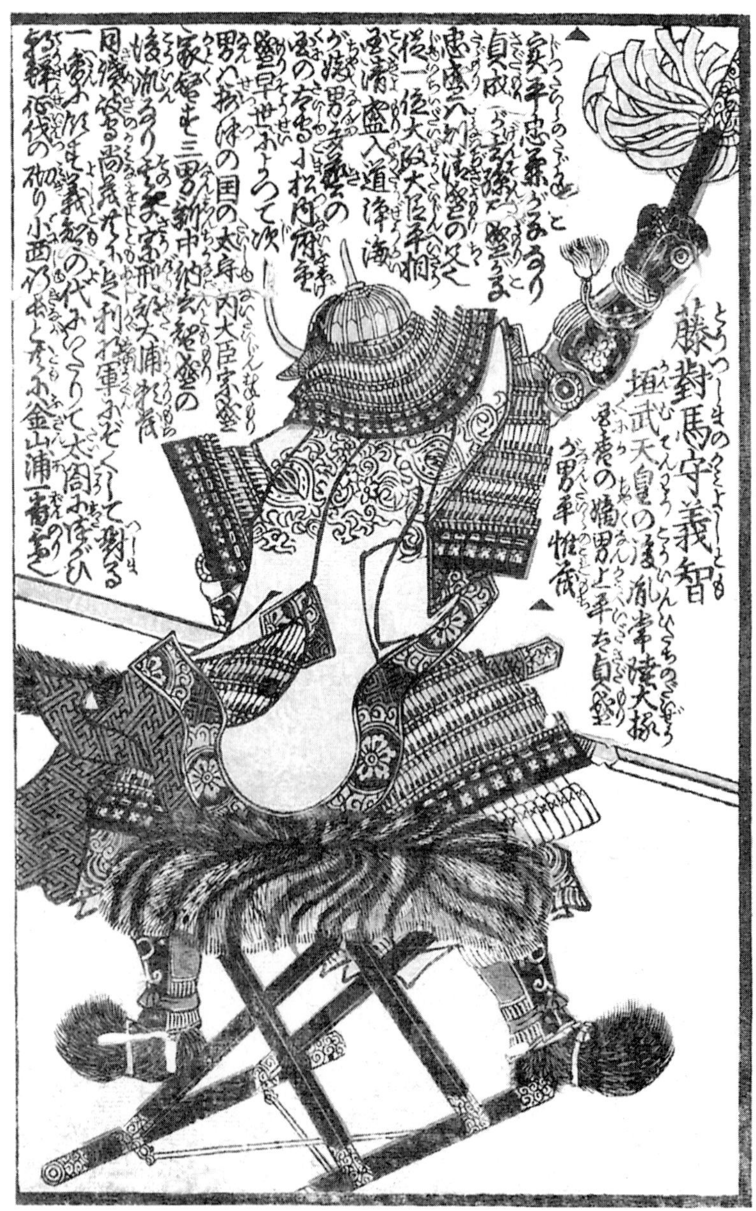

PLATE 64

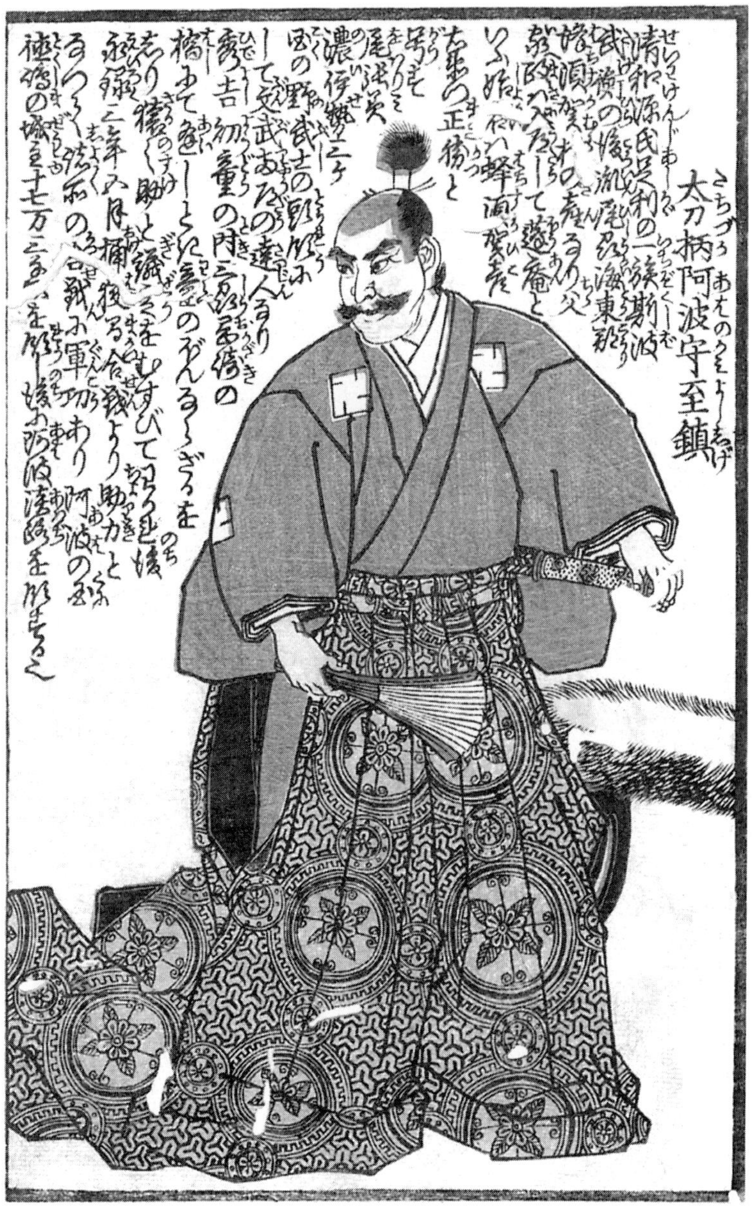

PLATE 65

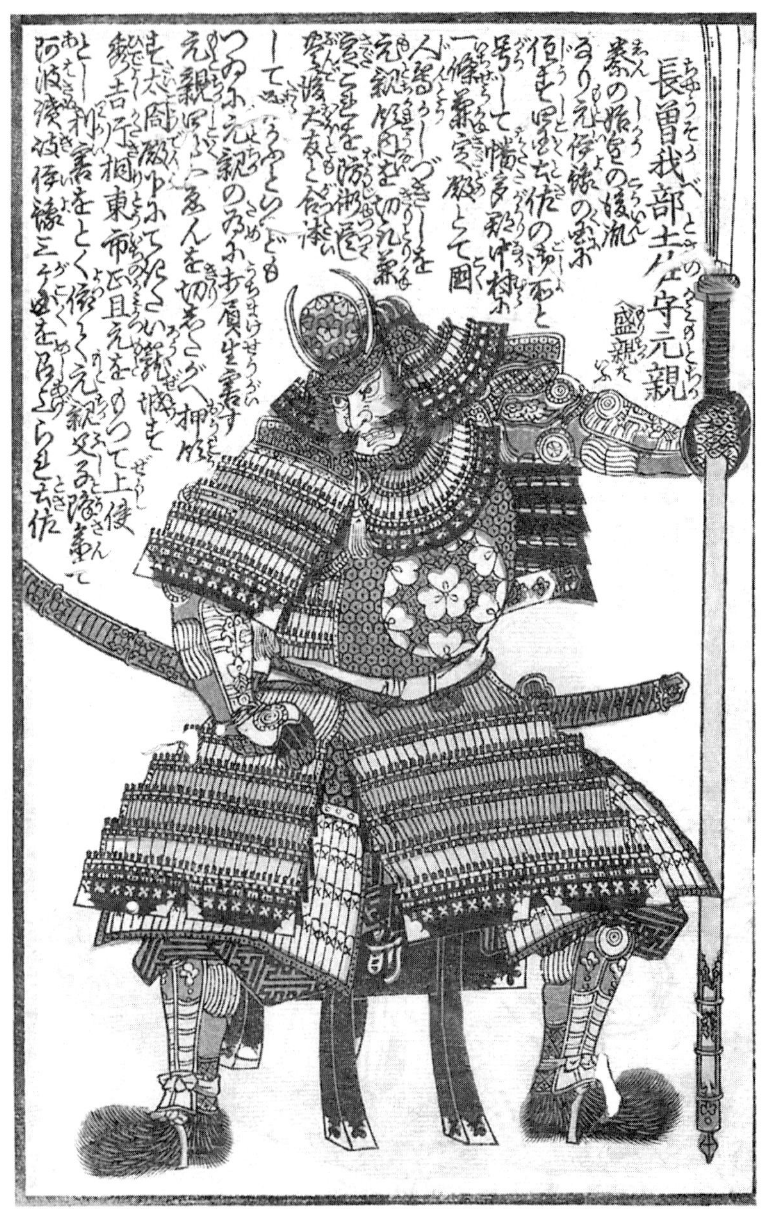

PLATE 66

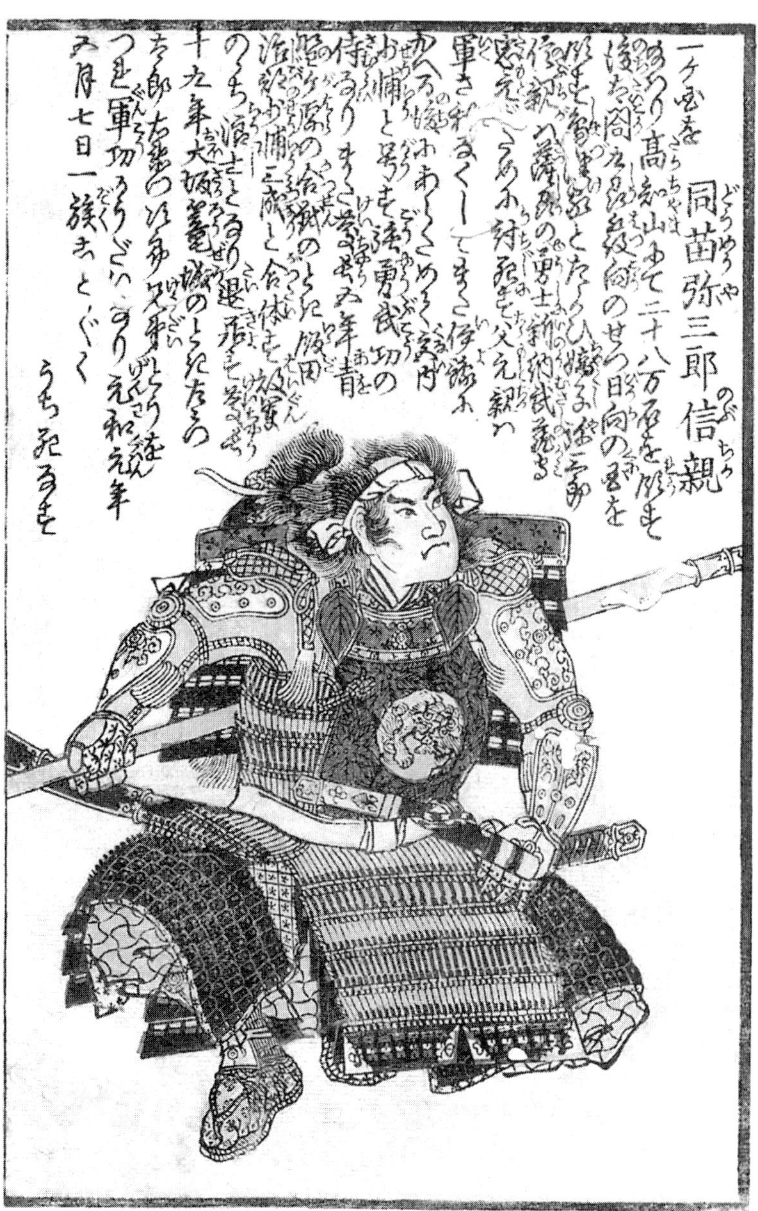

PLATE 67

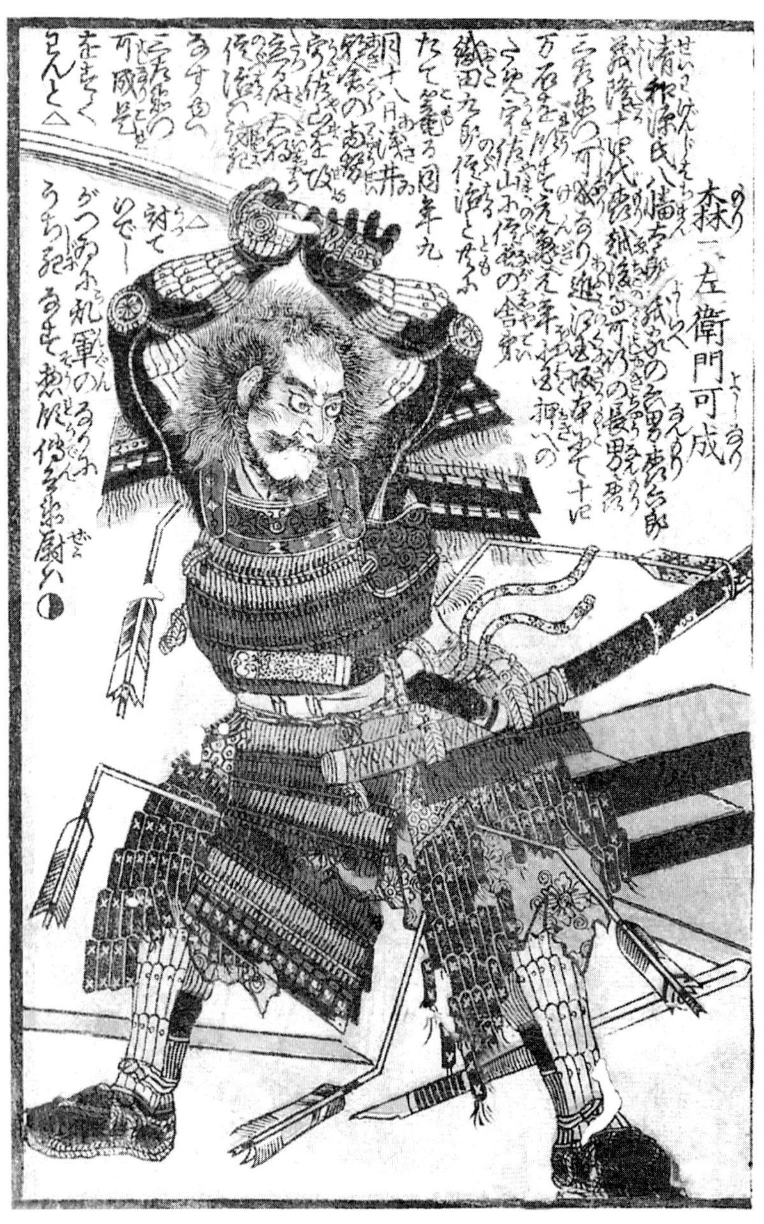

Plate 68

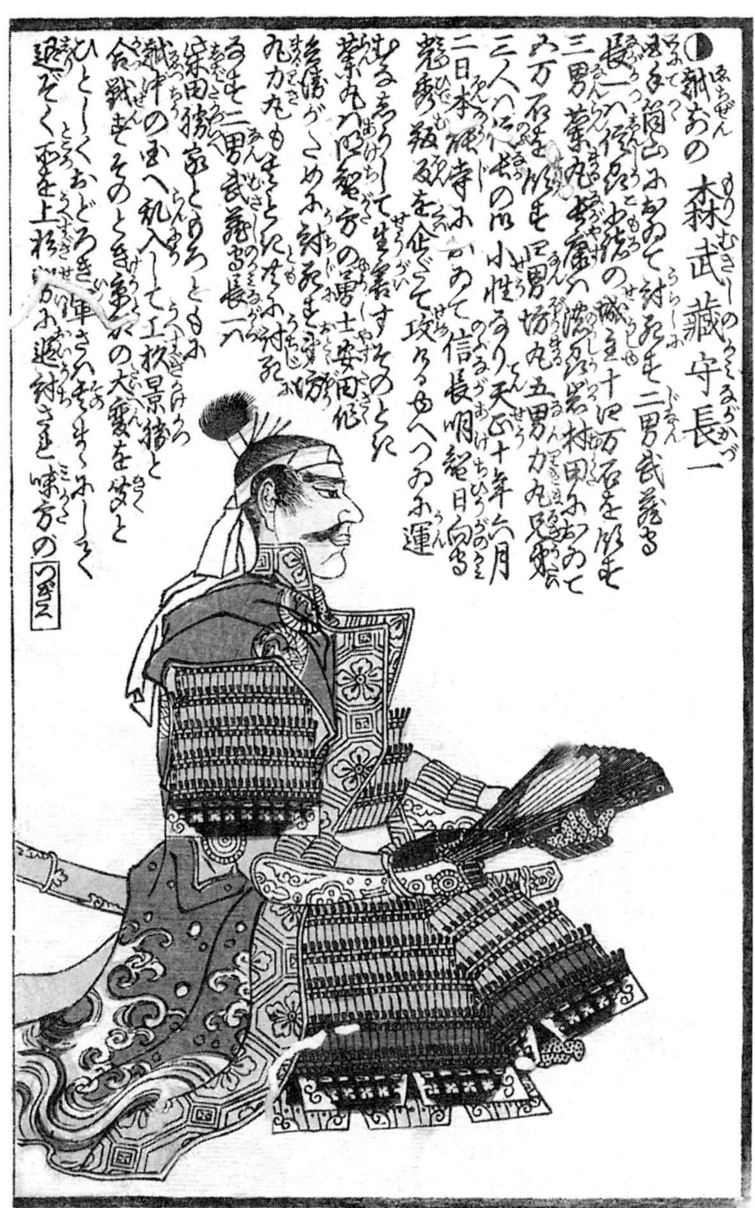

Plate 69

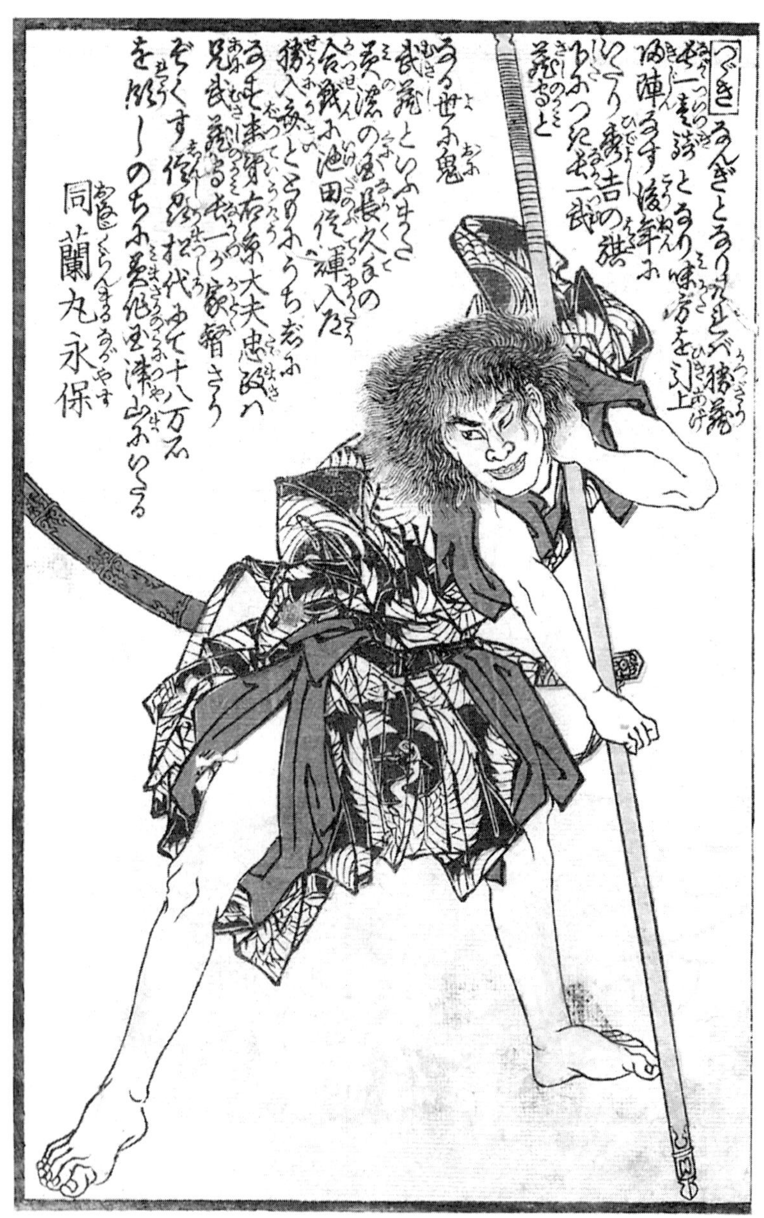

PLATE 70

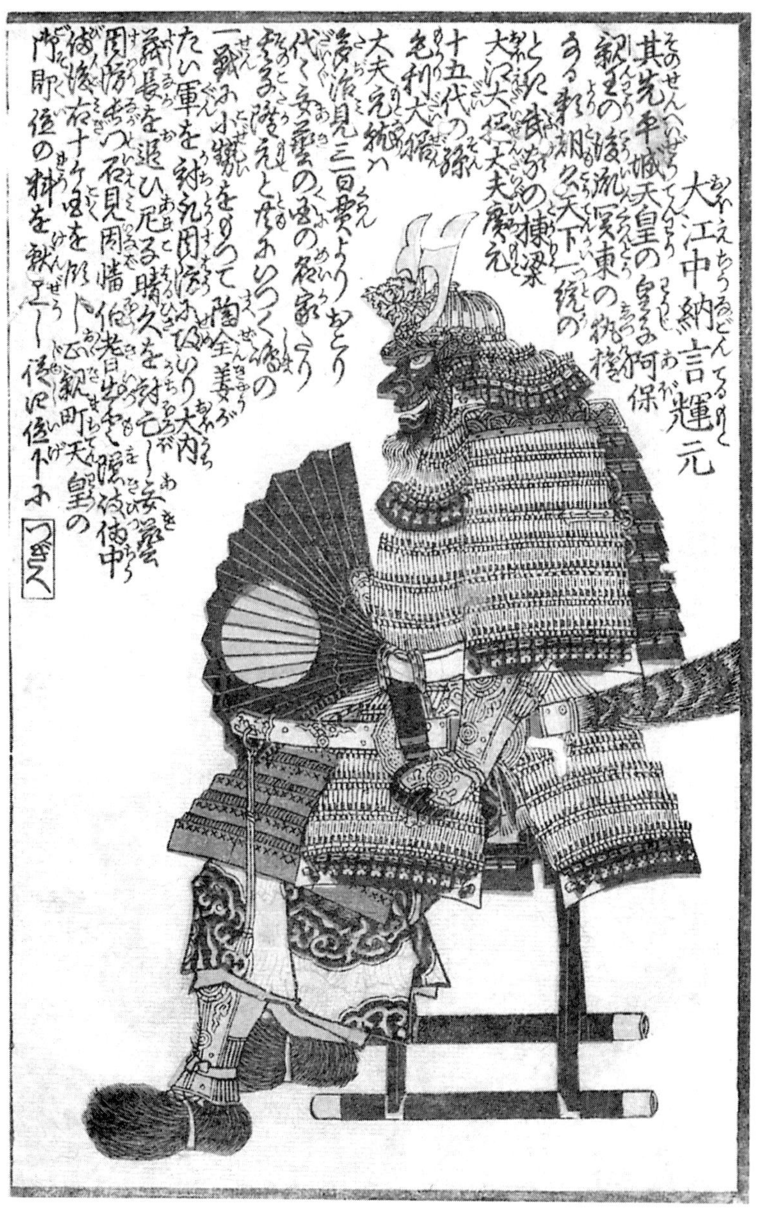

PLATE 71

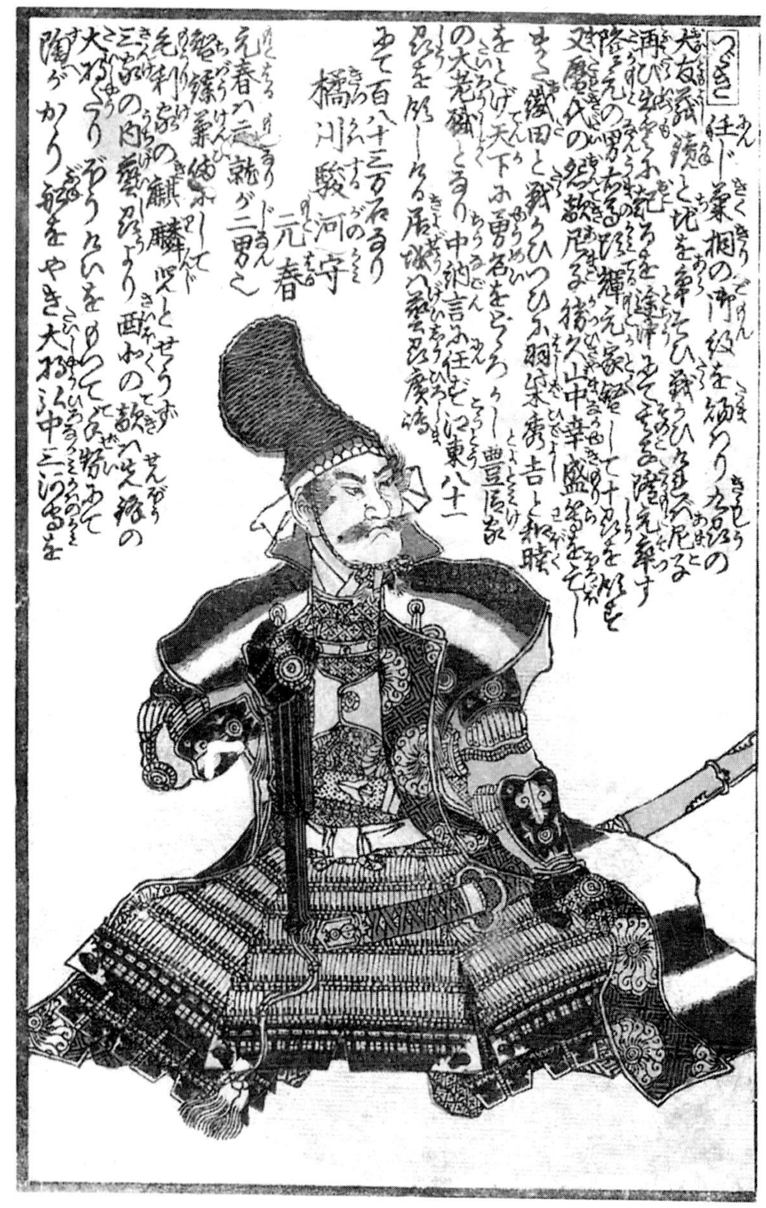

PLATE 72

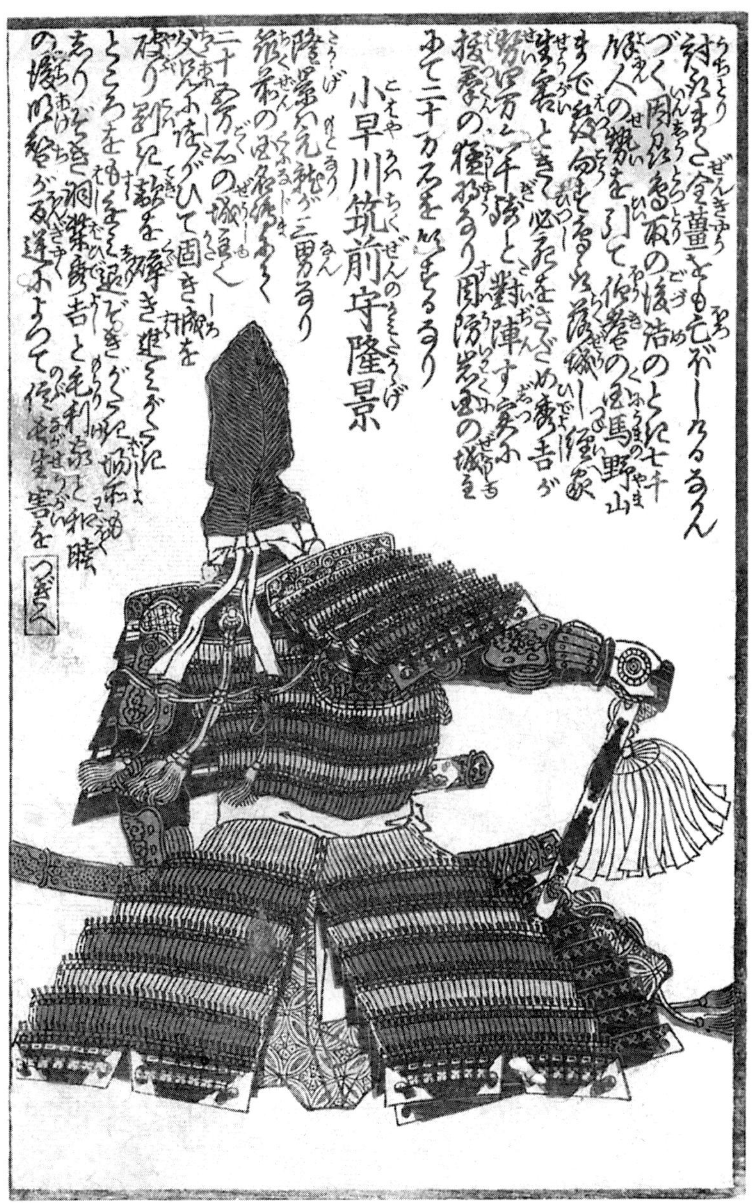

Plate 73

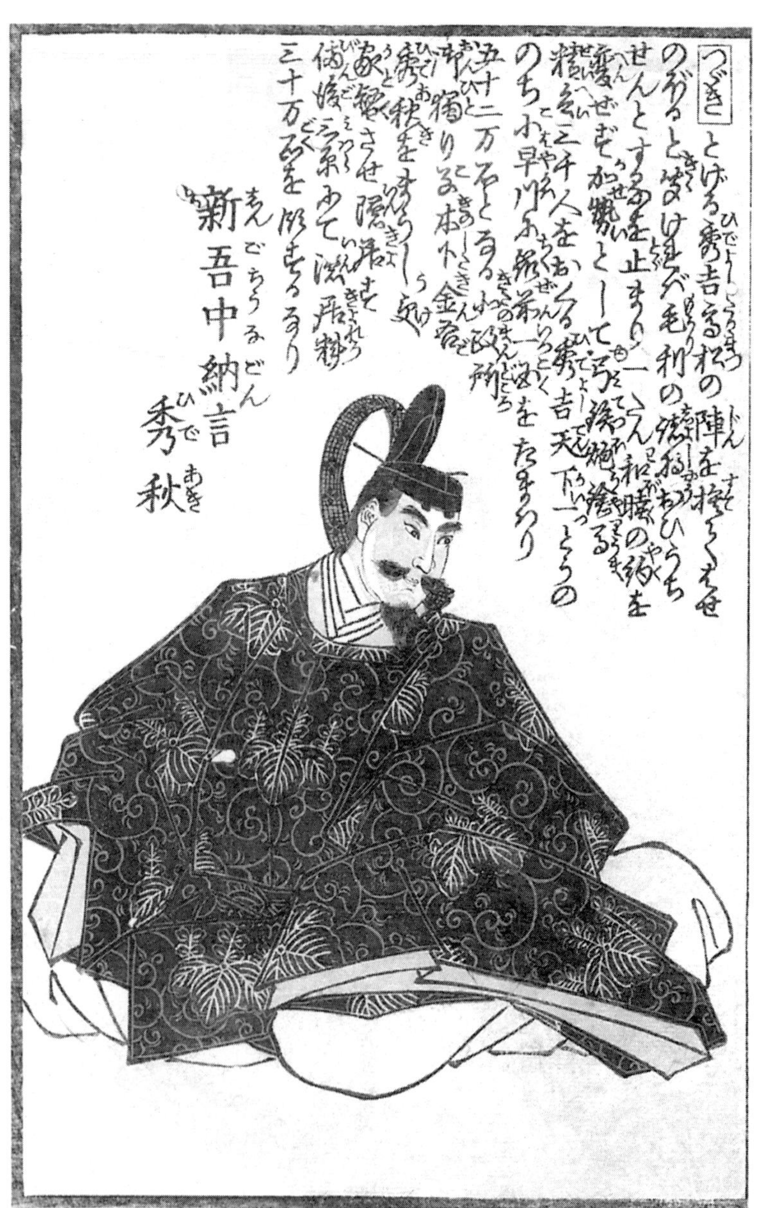

PLATE 74

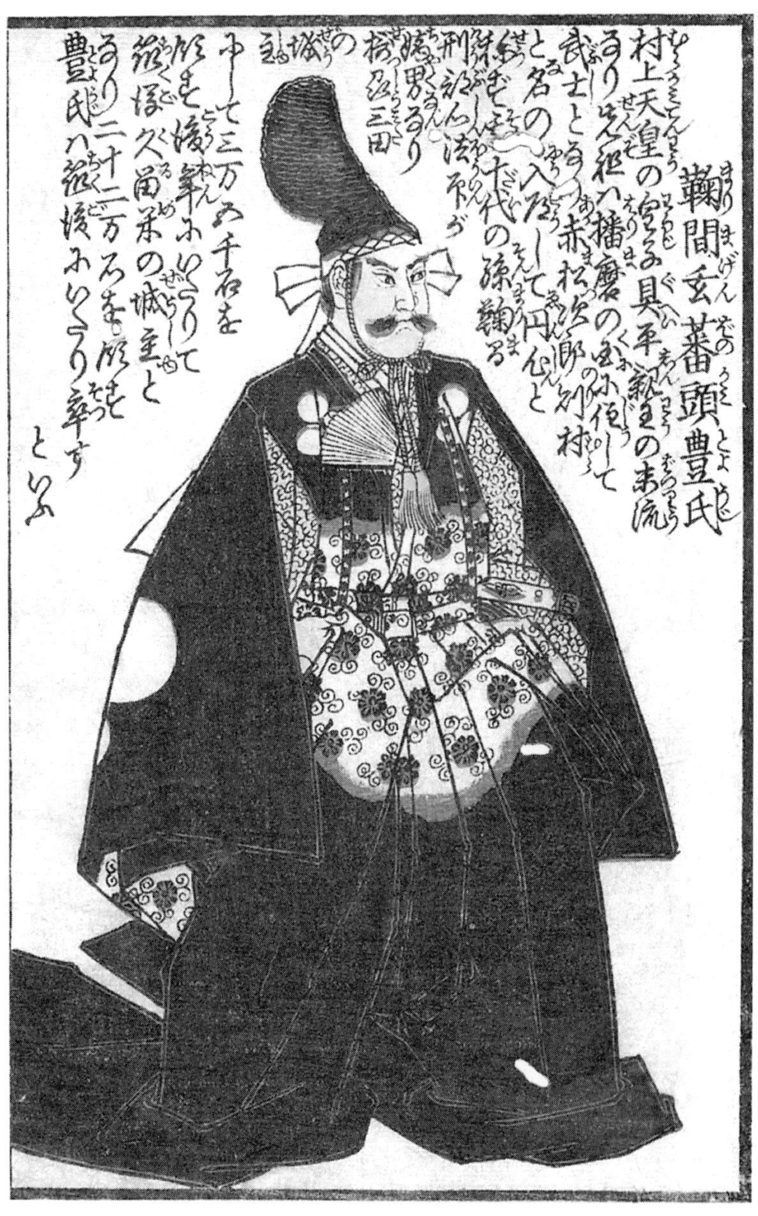

PLATE 75

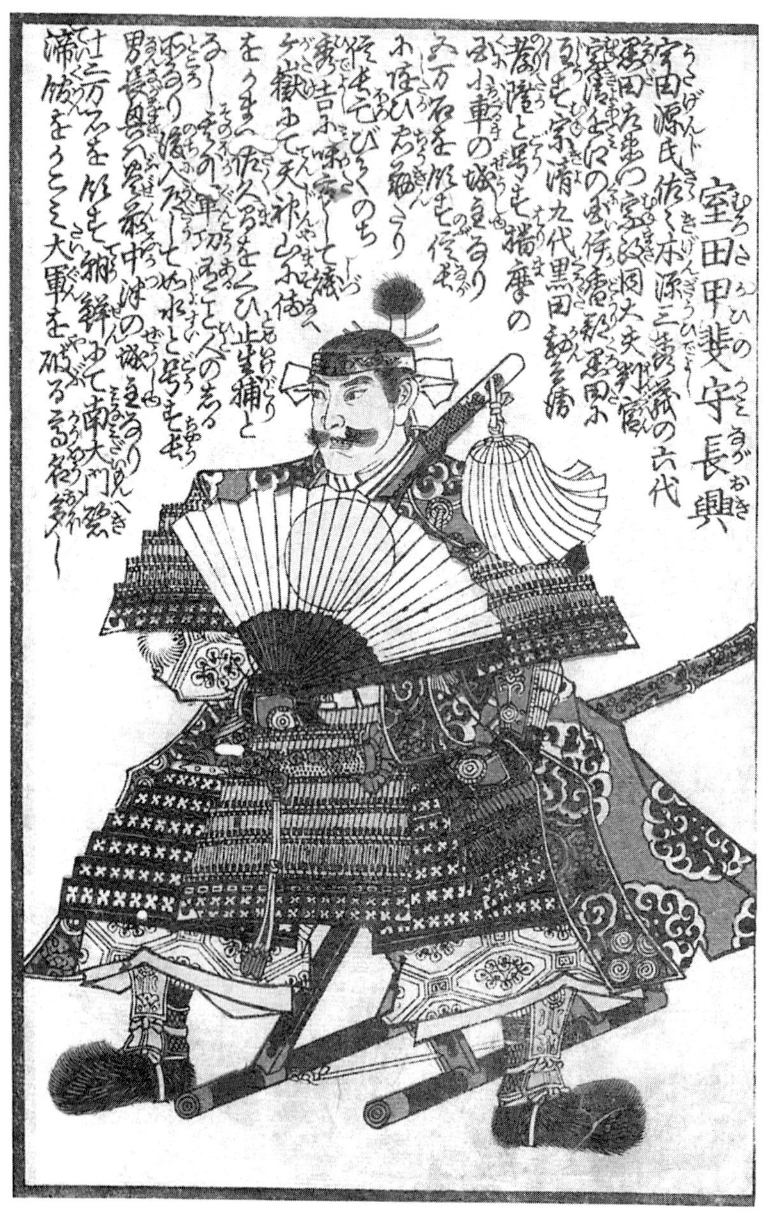

PLATE 76

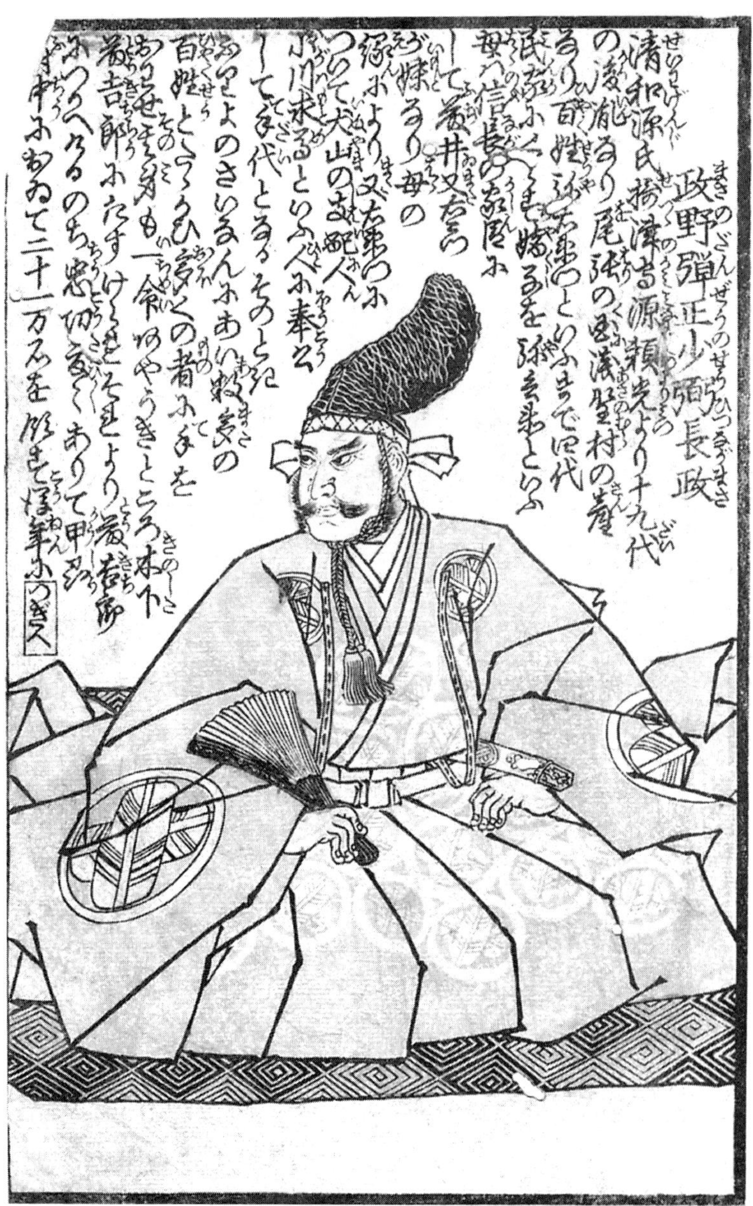

PLATE 77

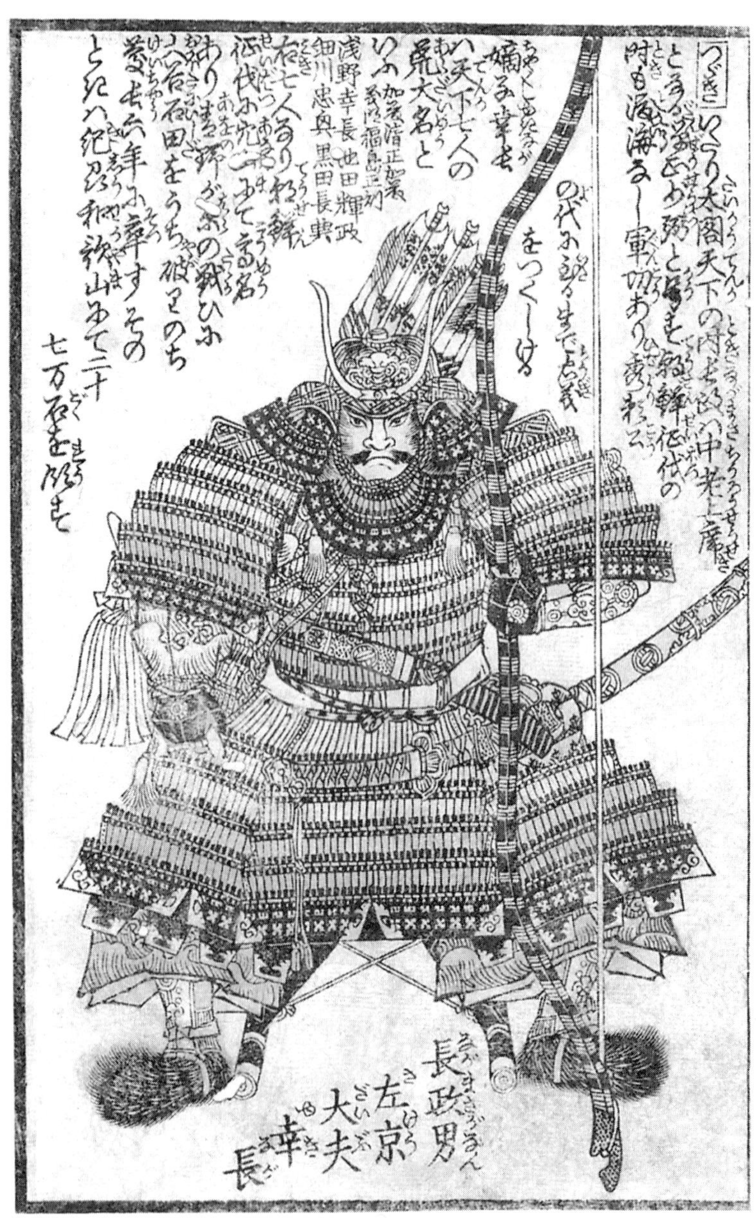

PLATE 78

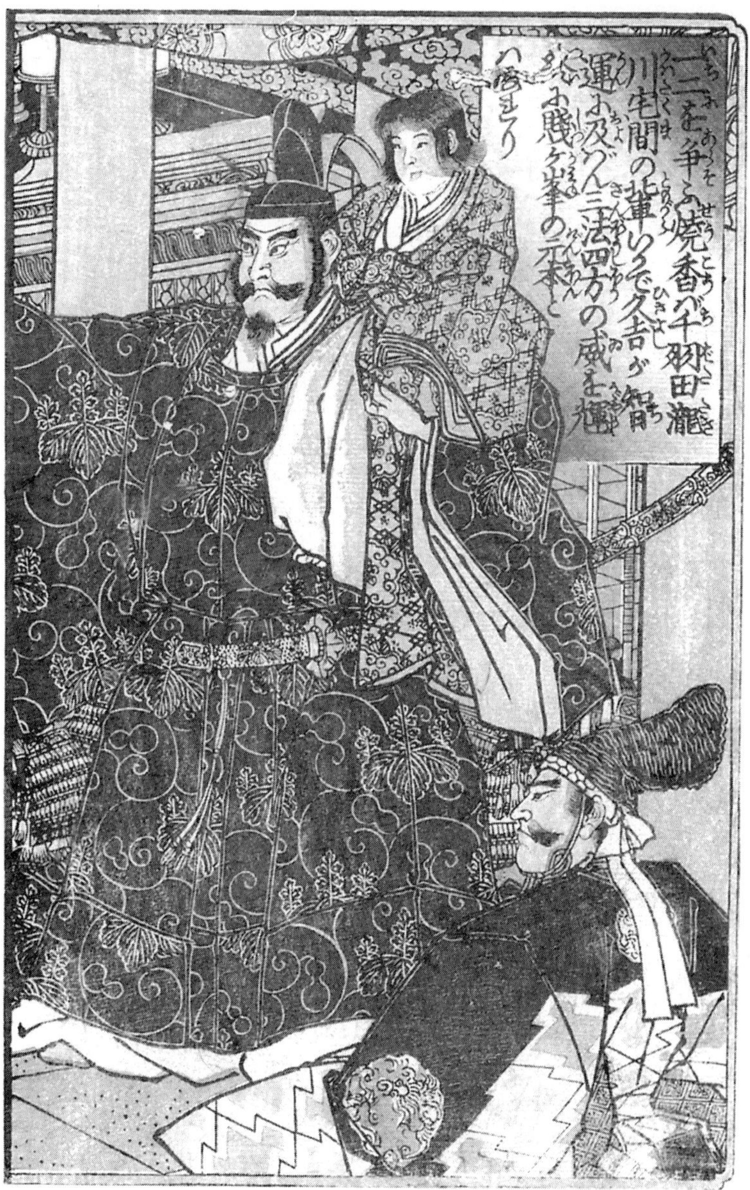

PLATE 79

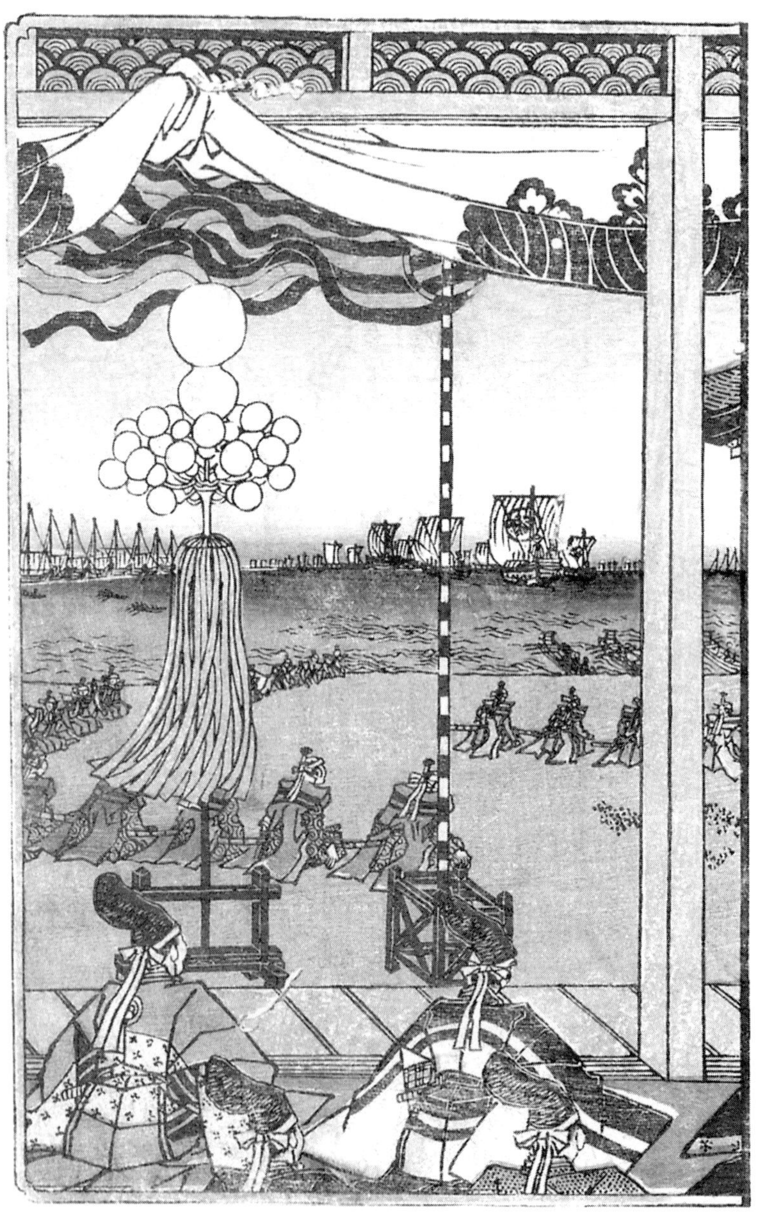

Plate 80

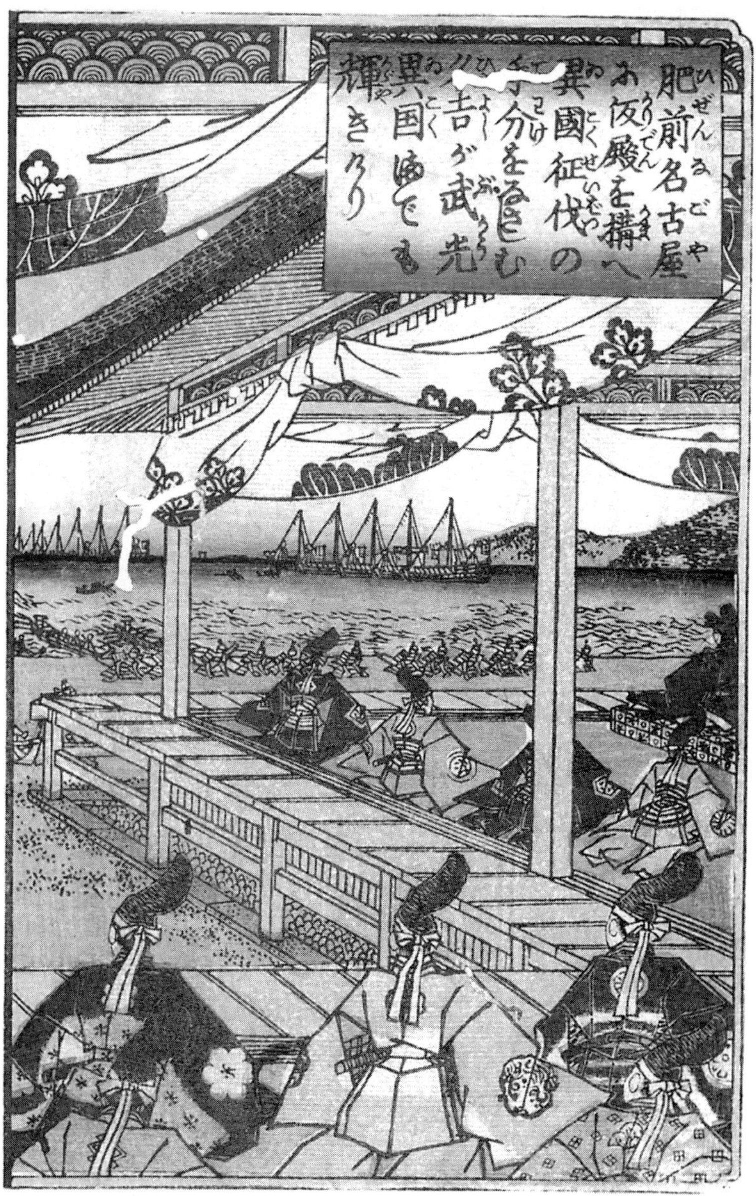

PLATE 81

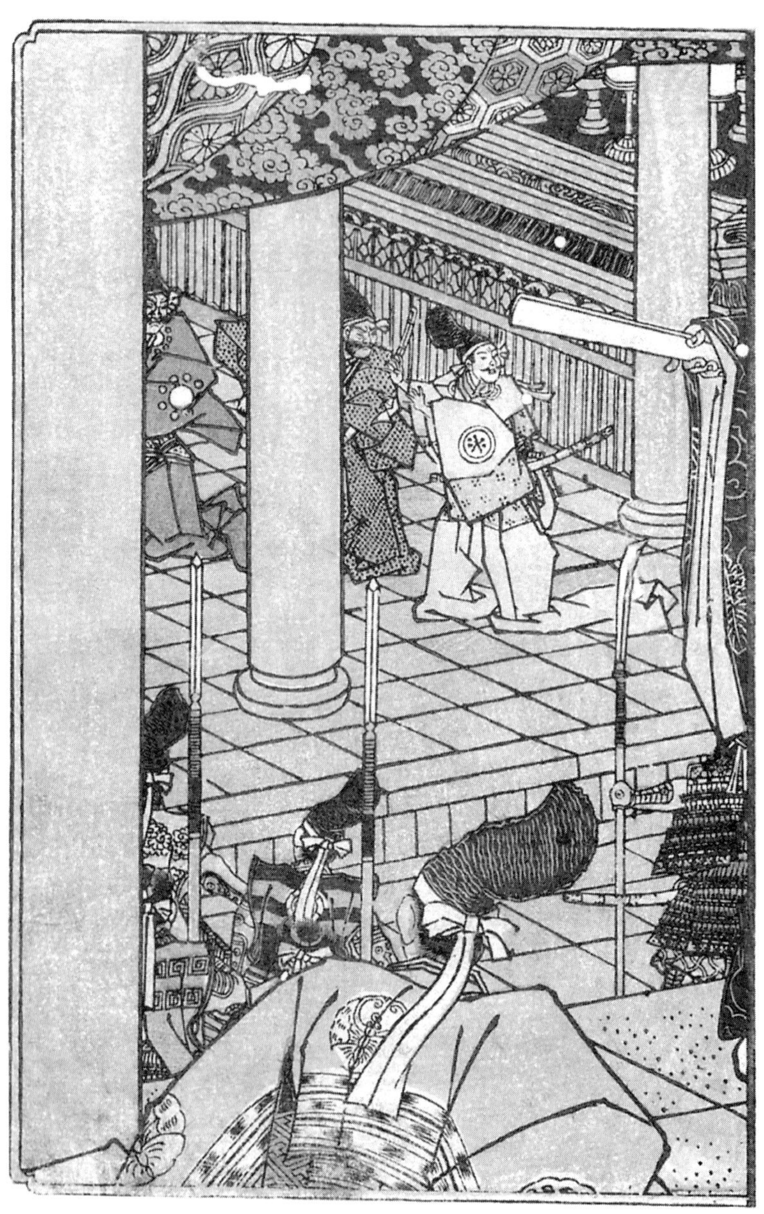

Plate 82

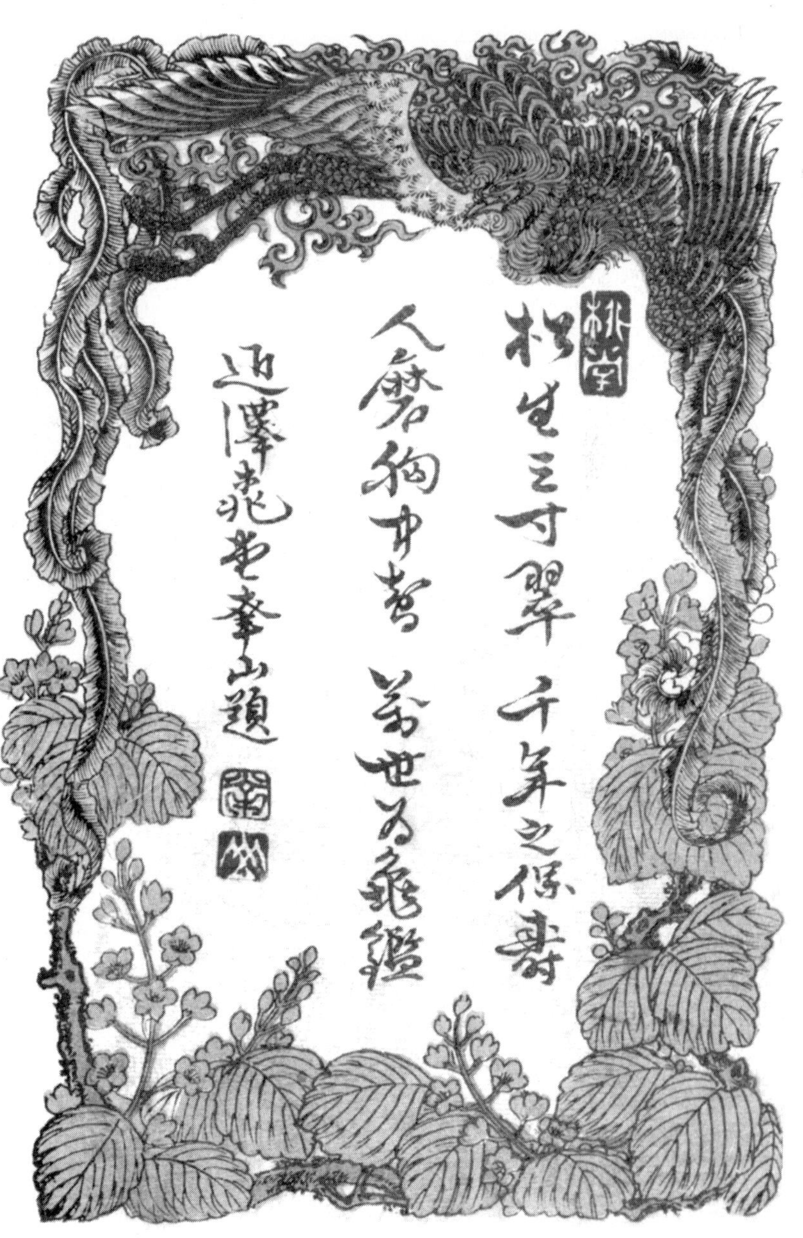

PLATE 83

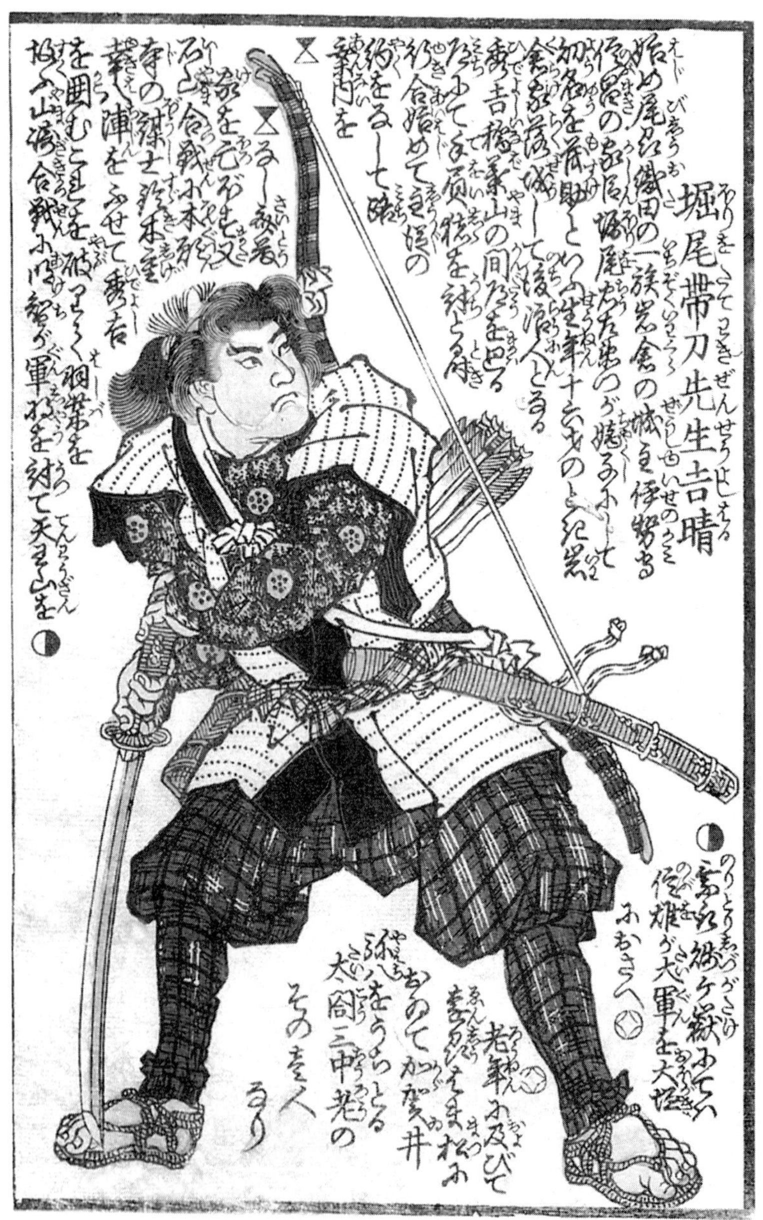

Plate 84

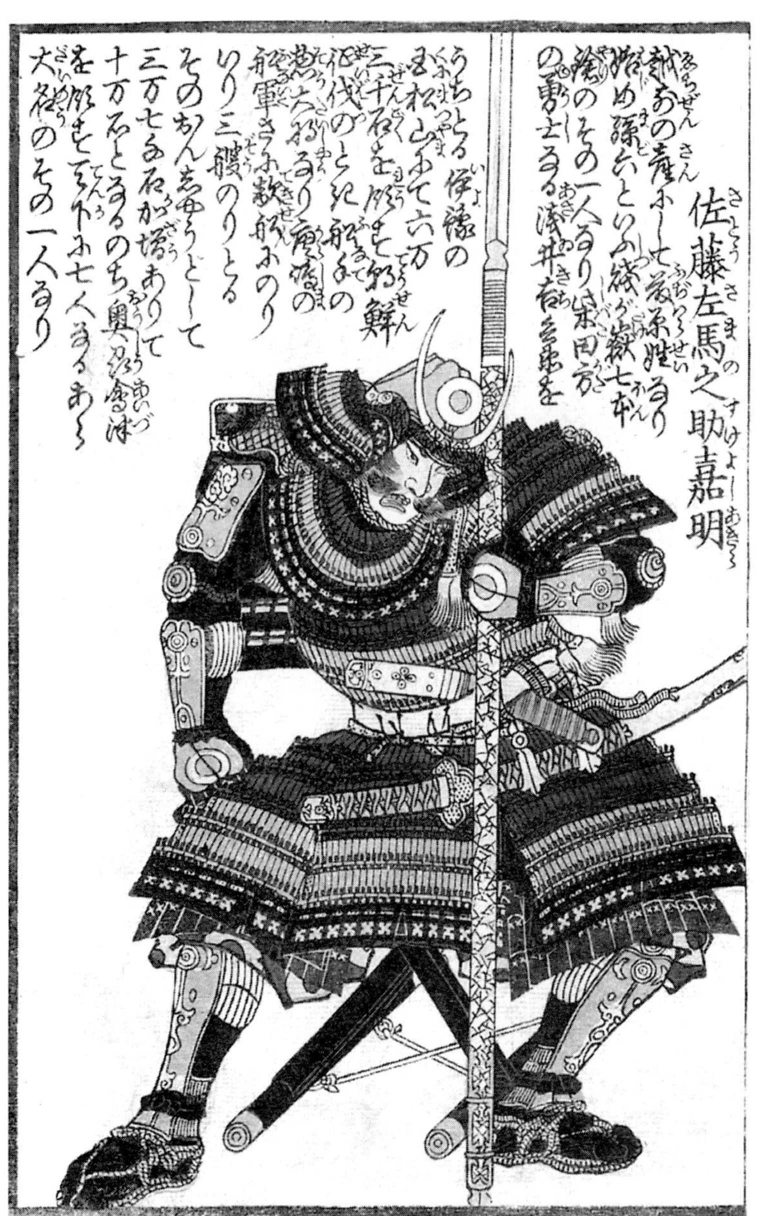

PLATE 85

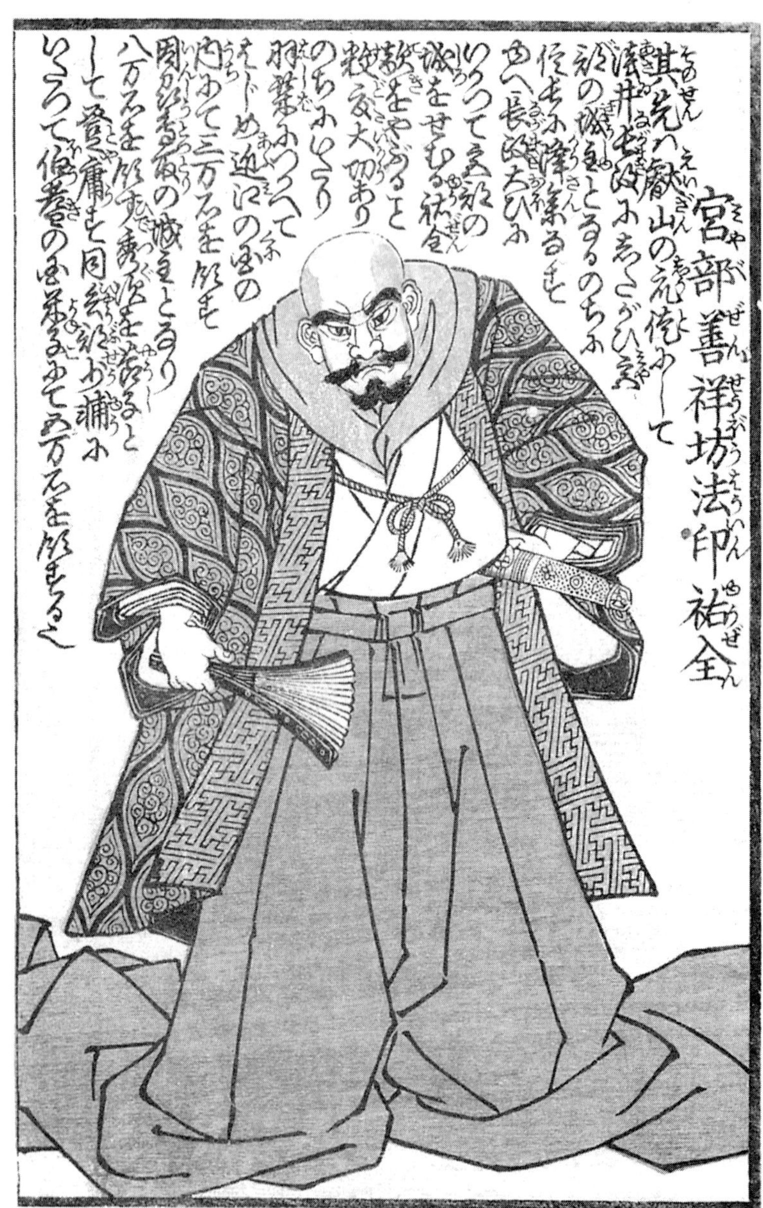

Plate 86

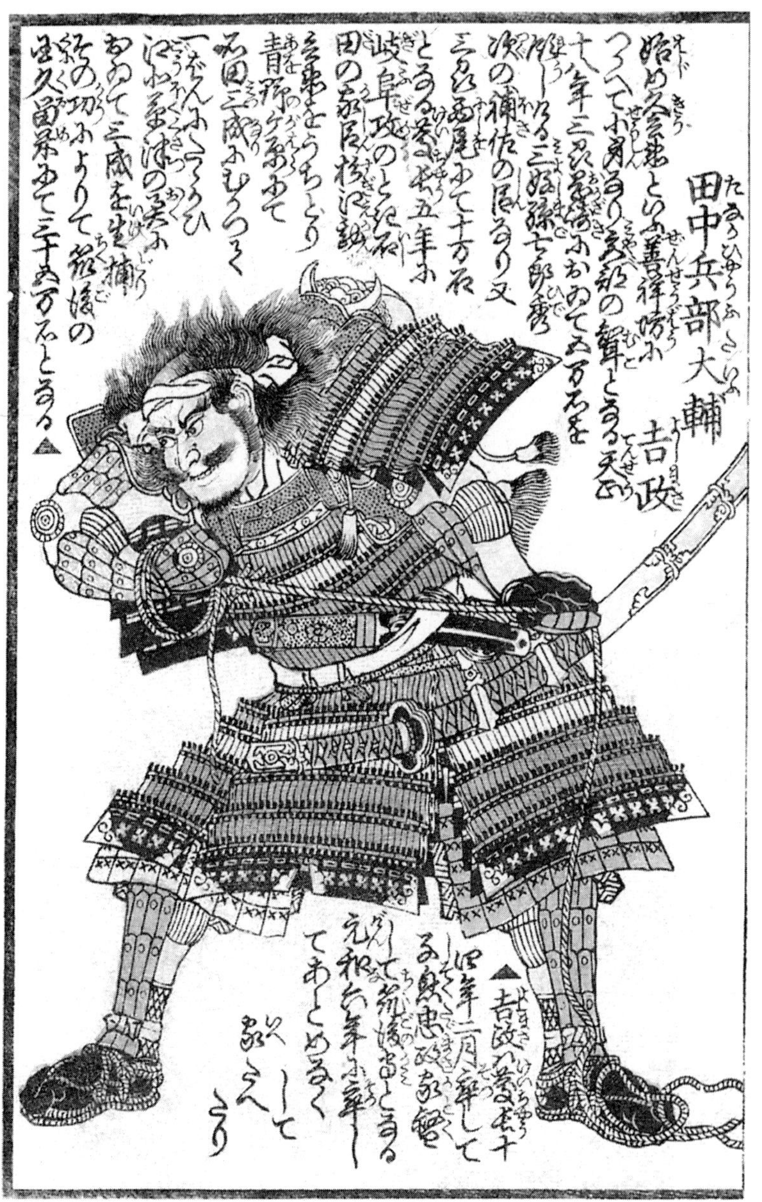

PLATE 87

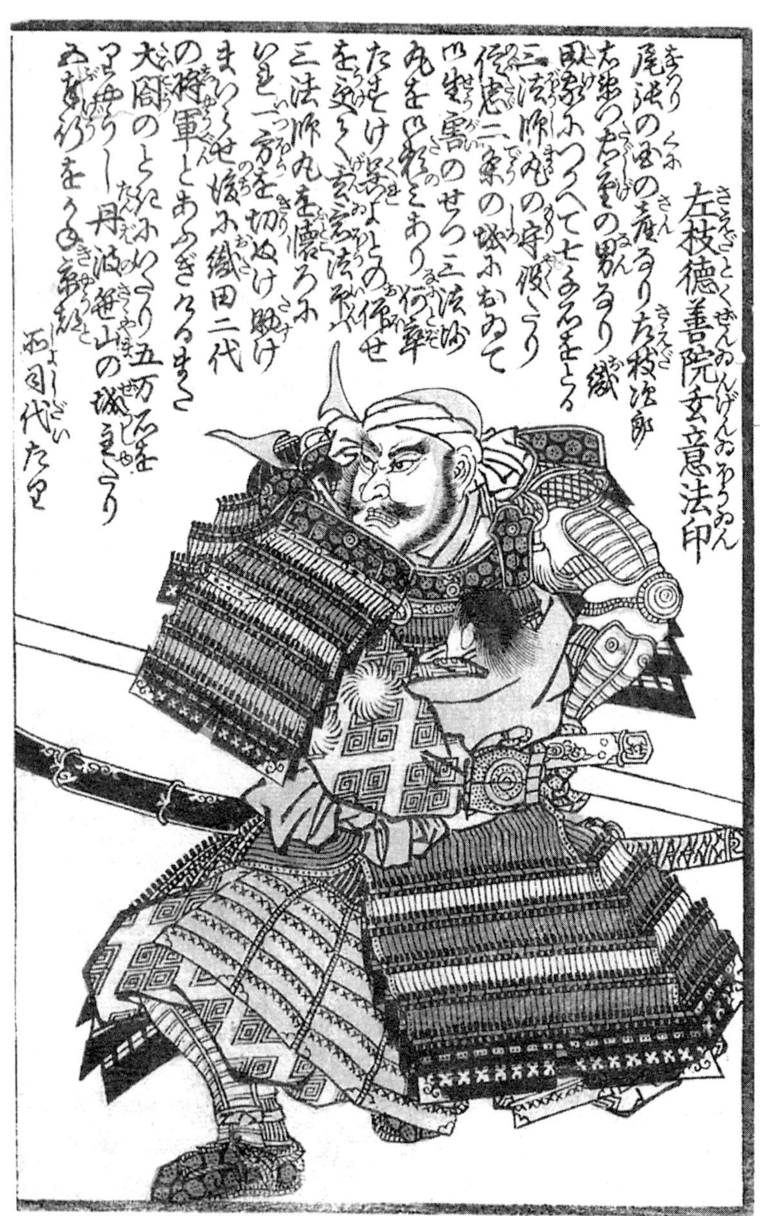

PLATE 88

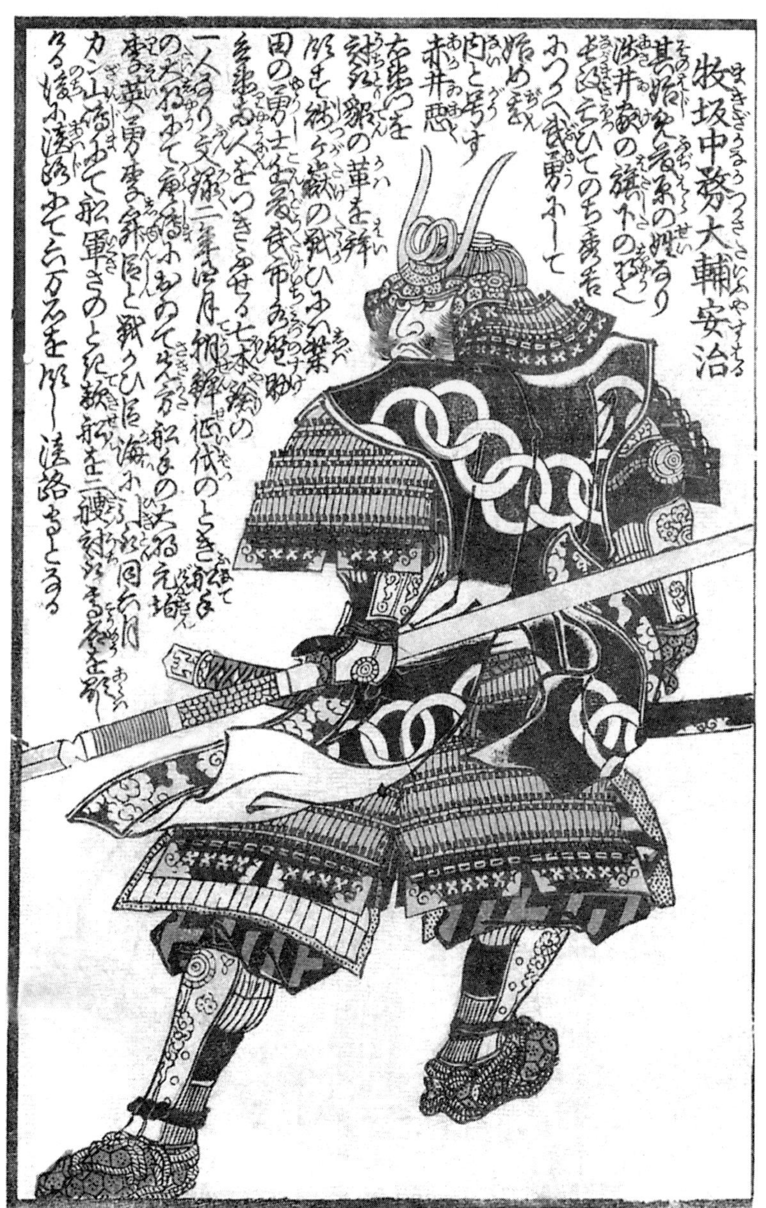

PLATE 89

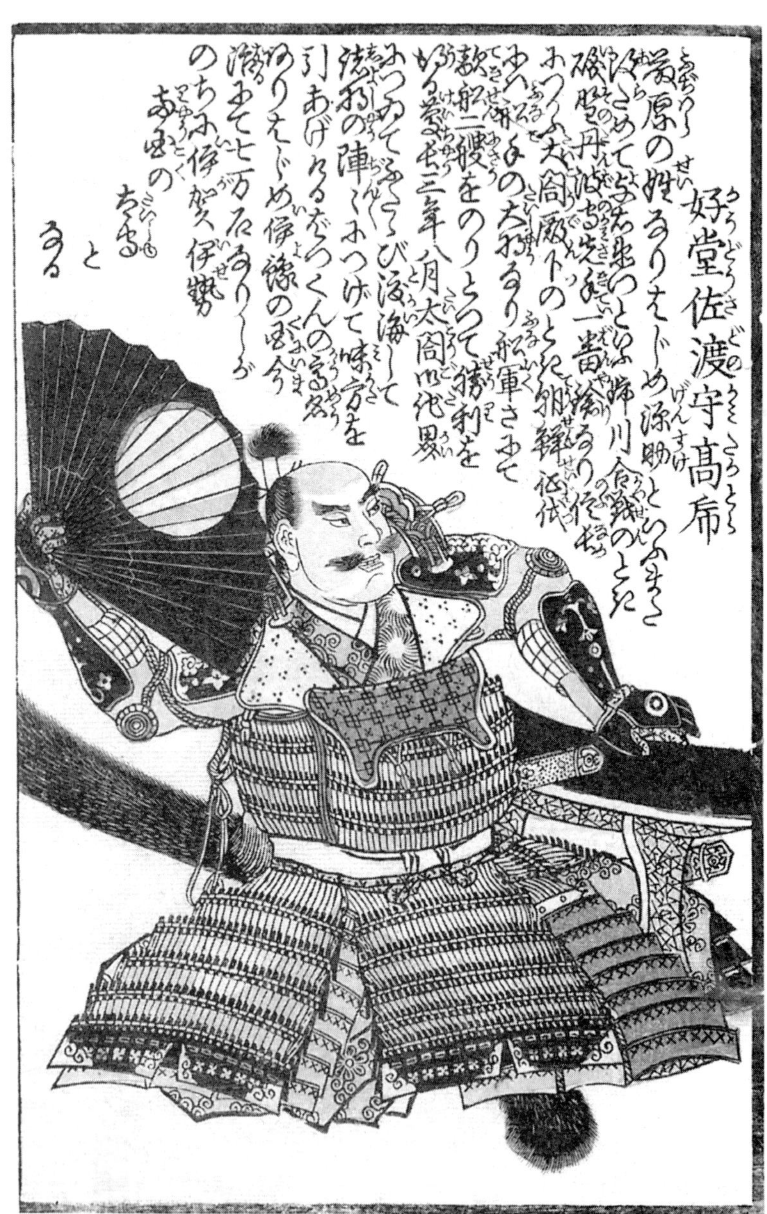

PLATE 90

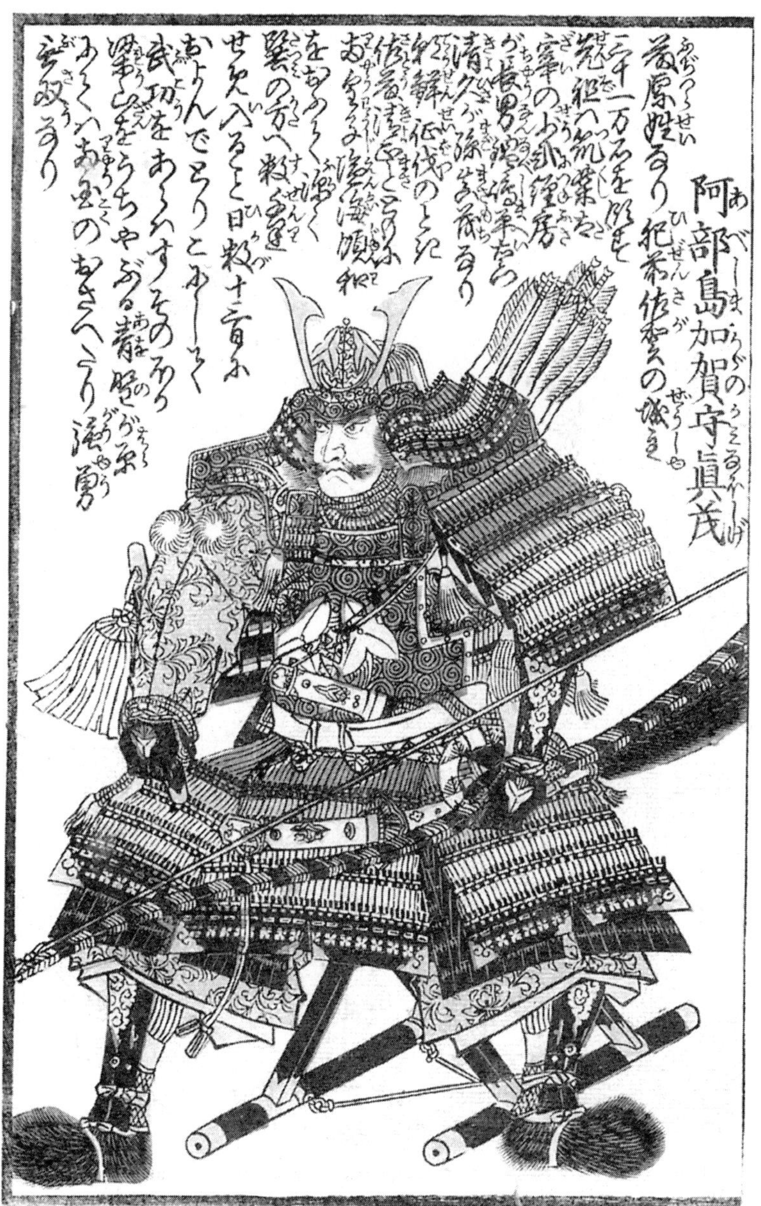

Plate 91

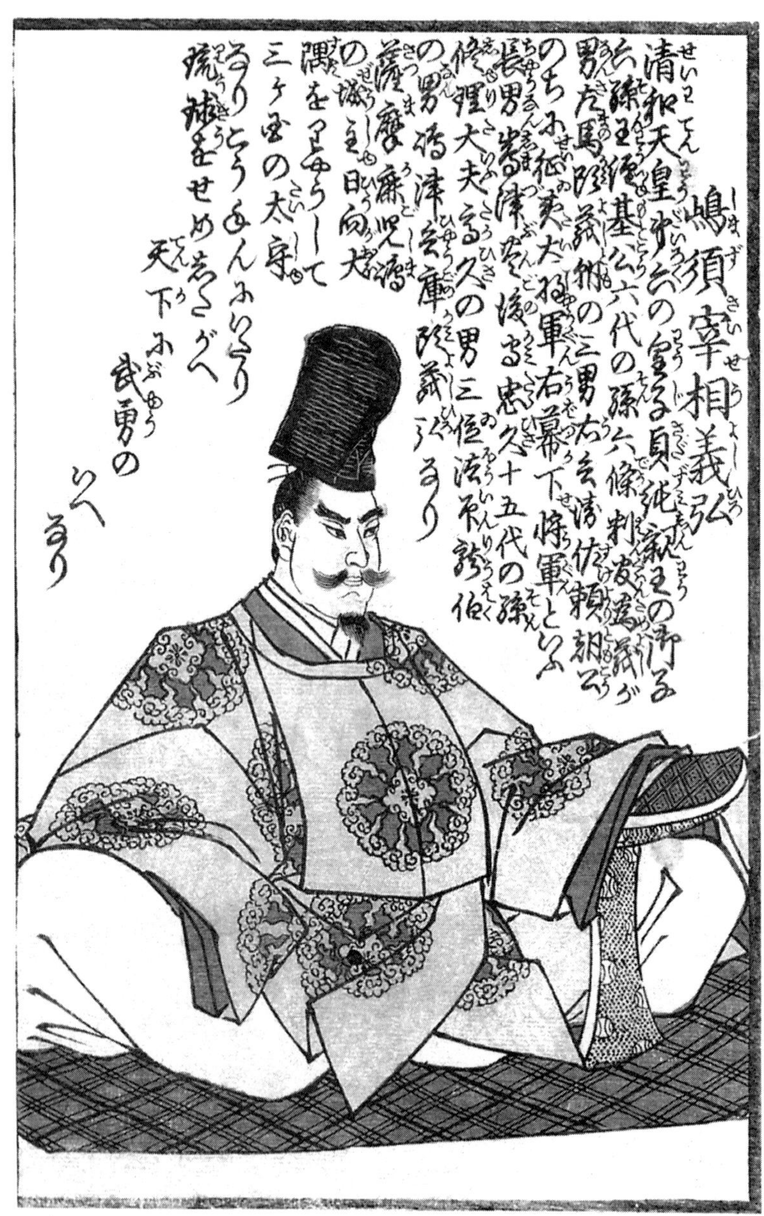

PLATE 92

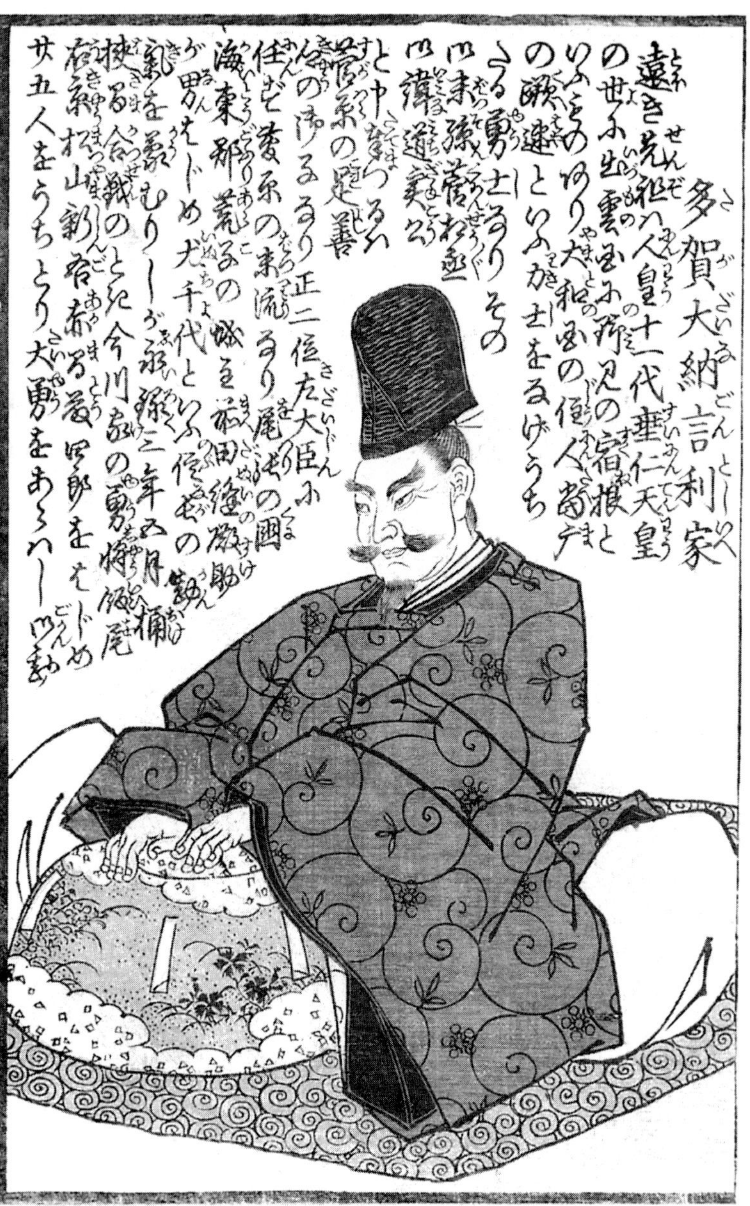

PLATE 93

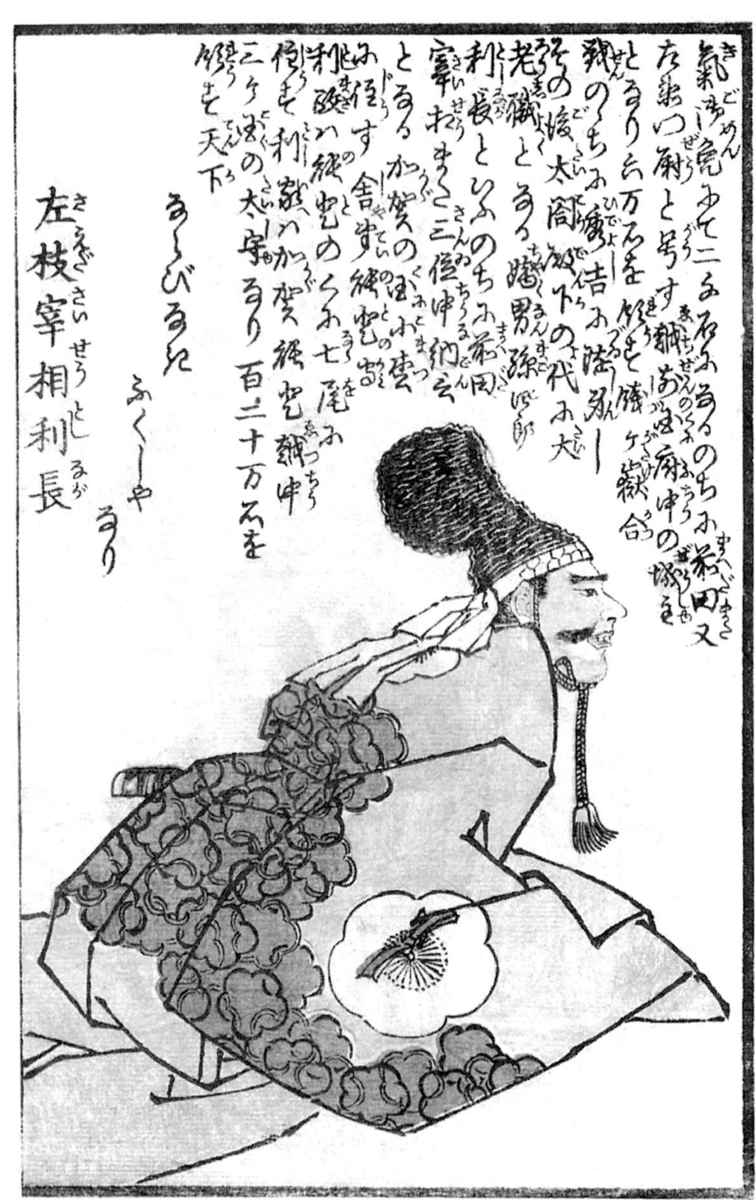

PLATE 94

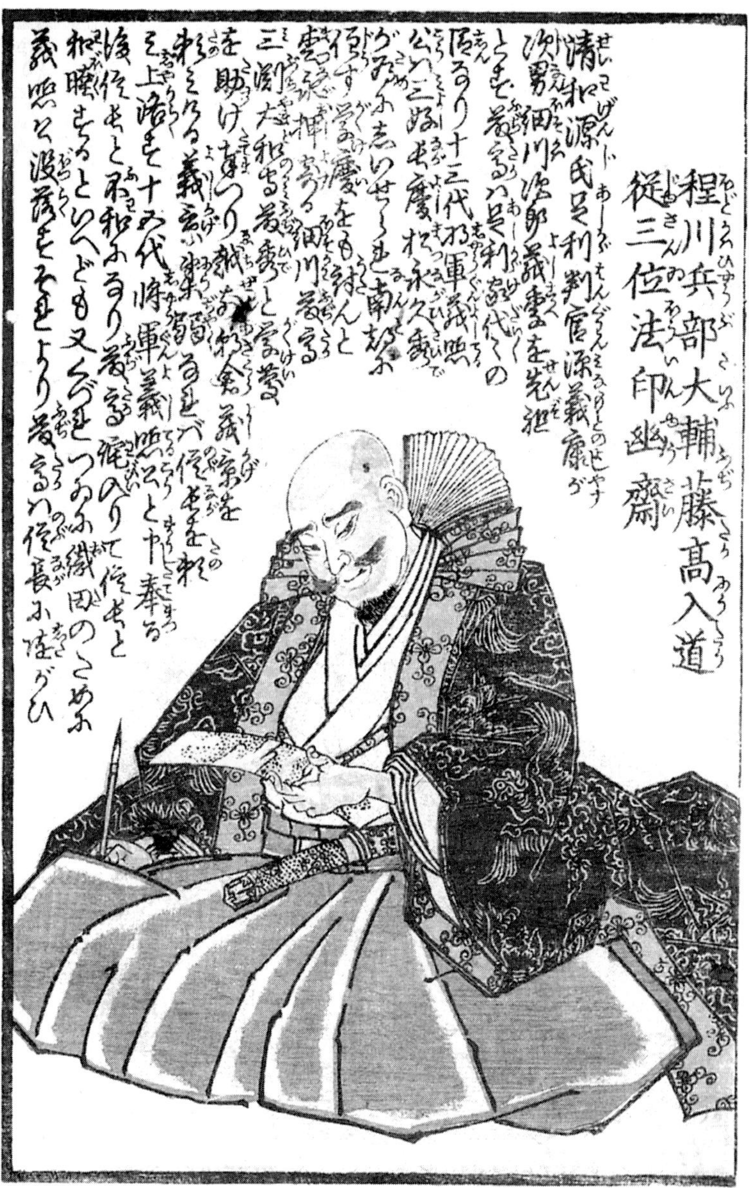

PLATE 95

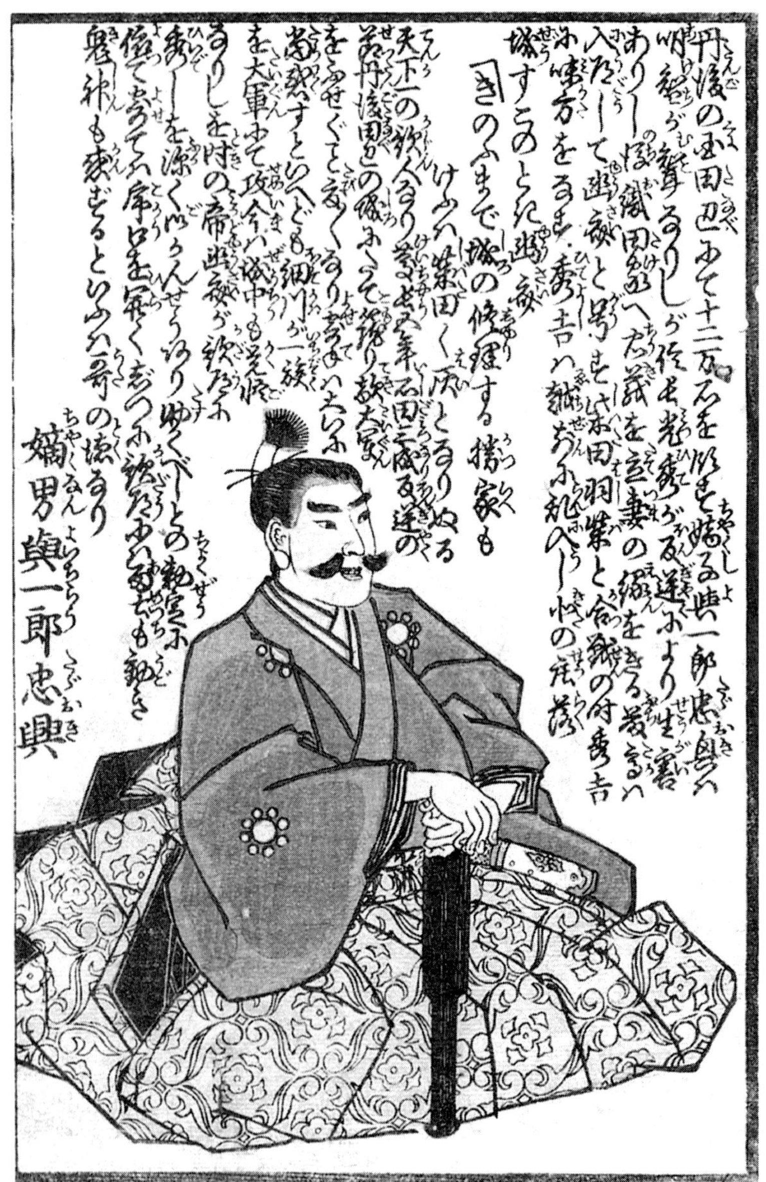

PLATE 96

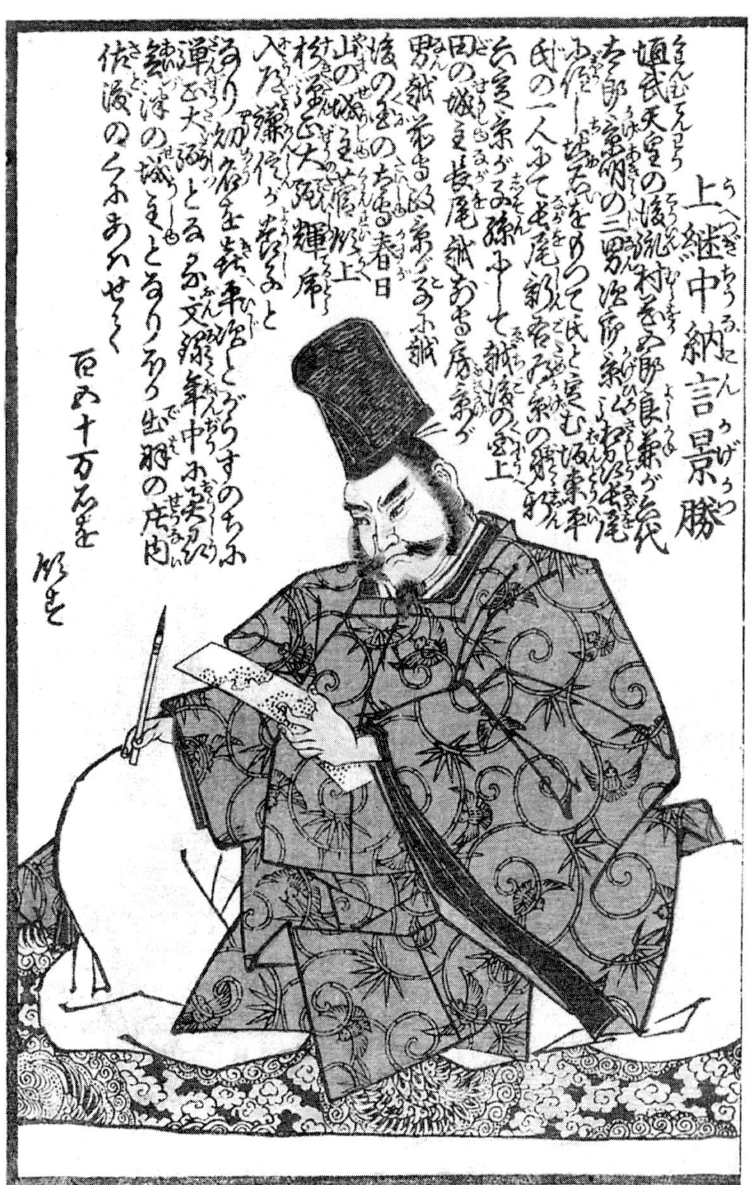

PLATE 97

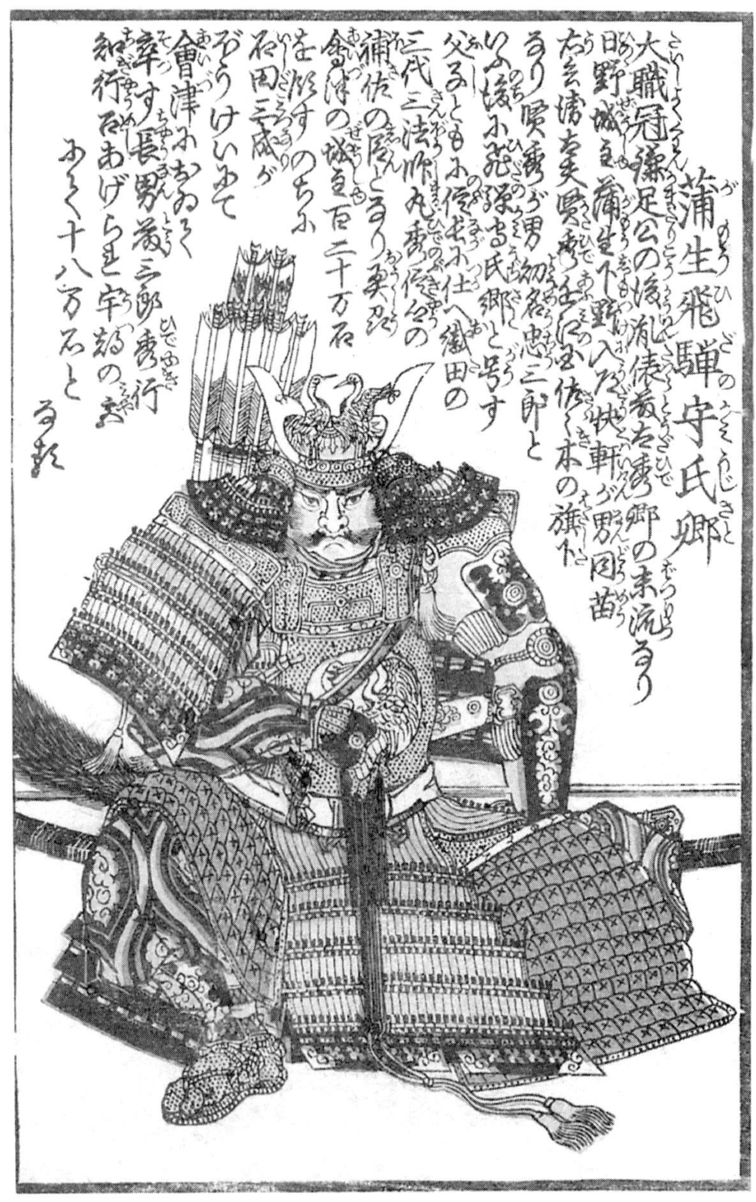

PLATE 98

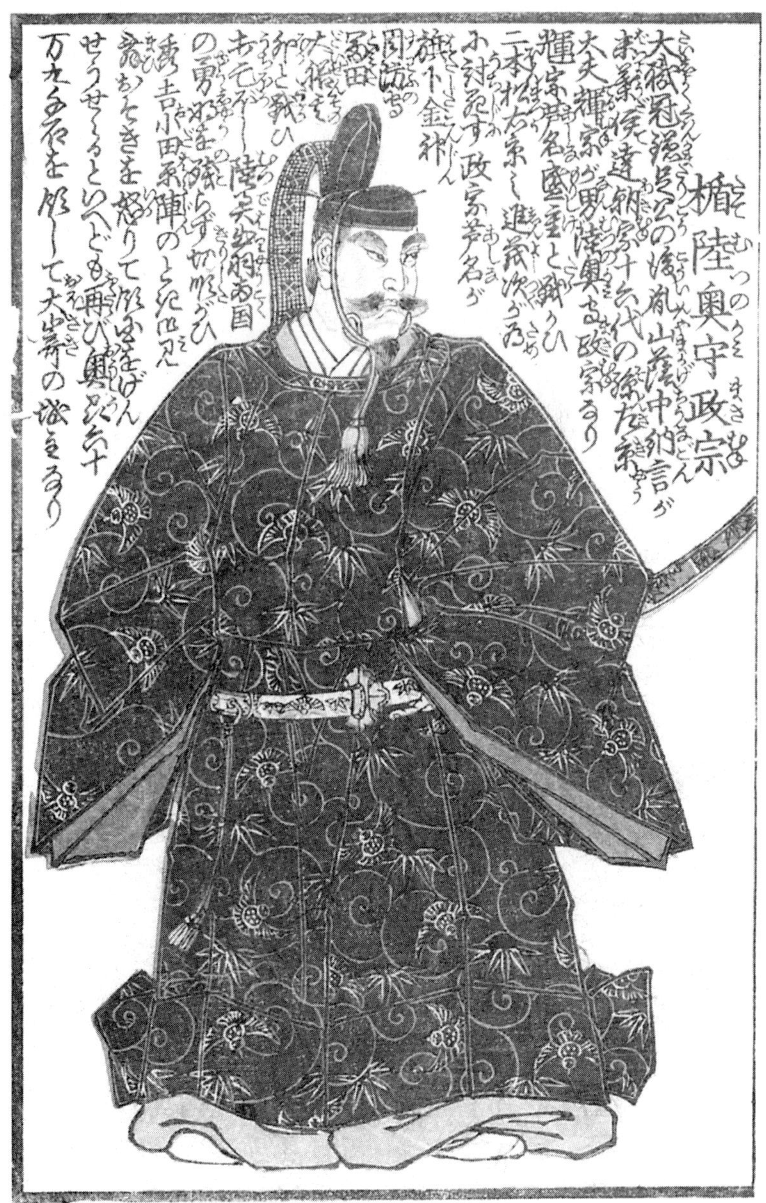

PLATE 99

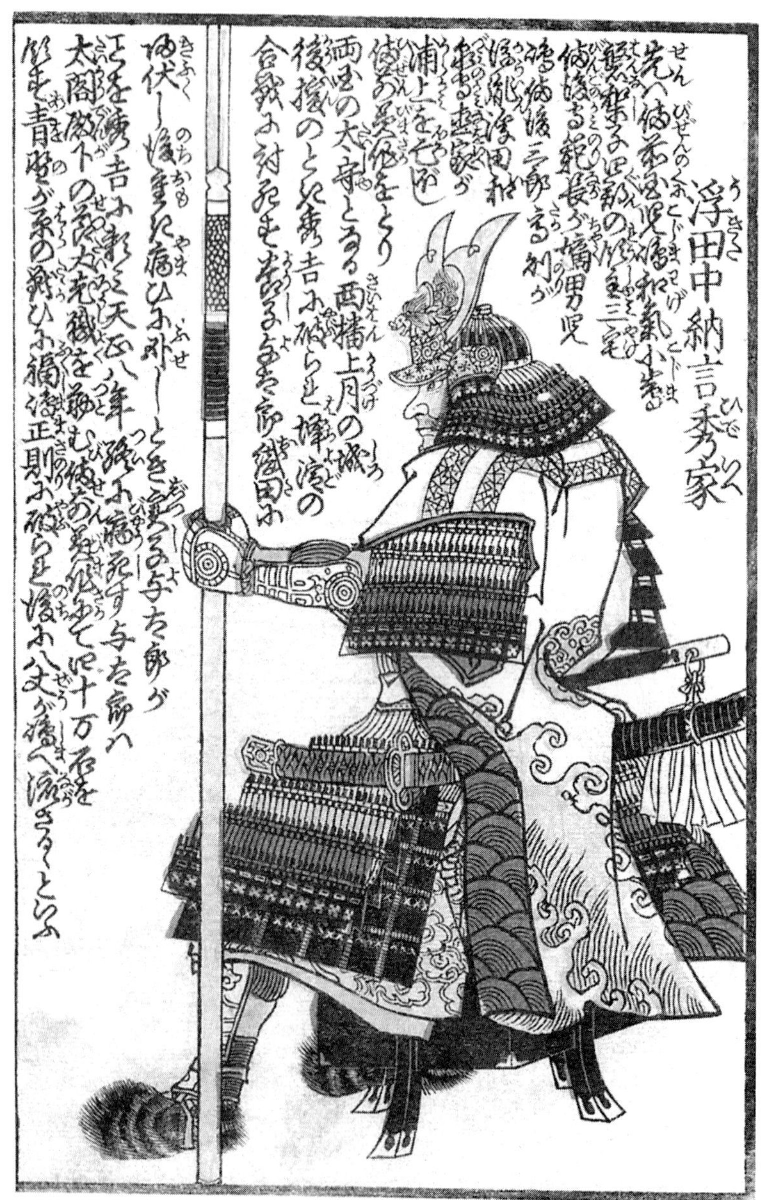

PLATE 100

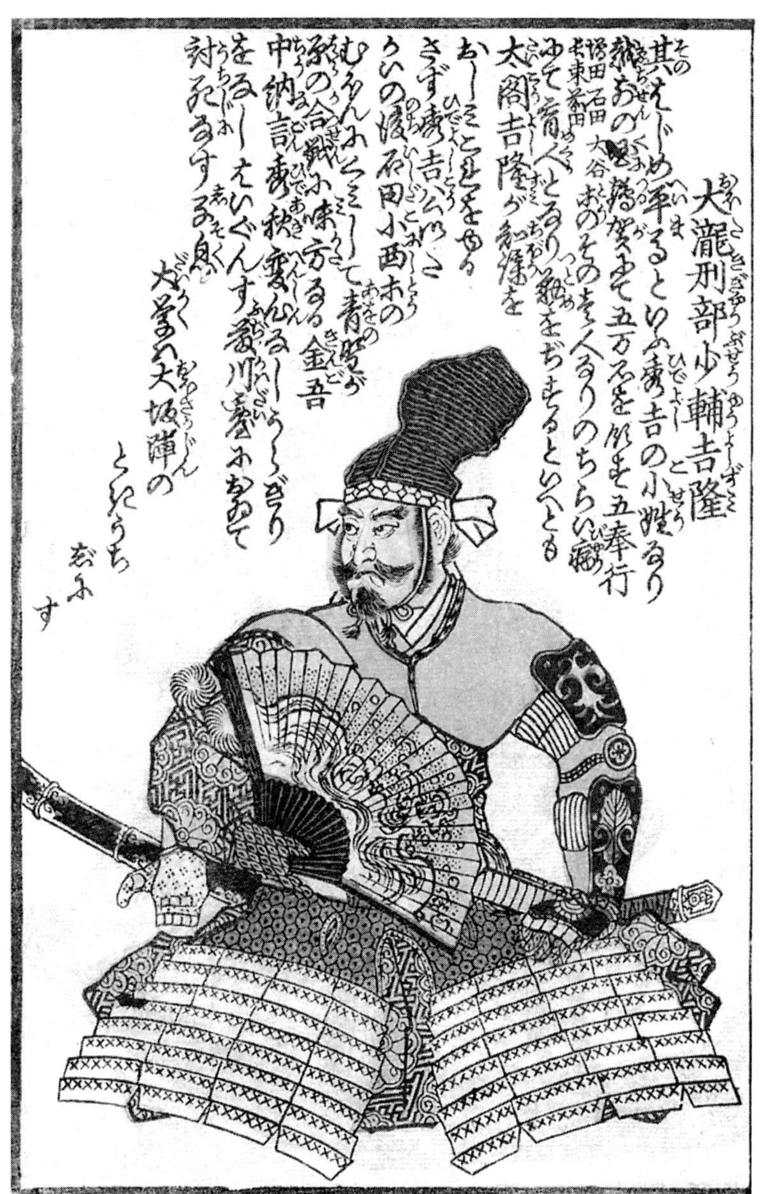

PLATE 101

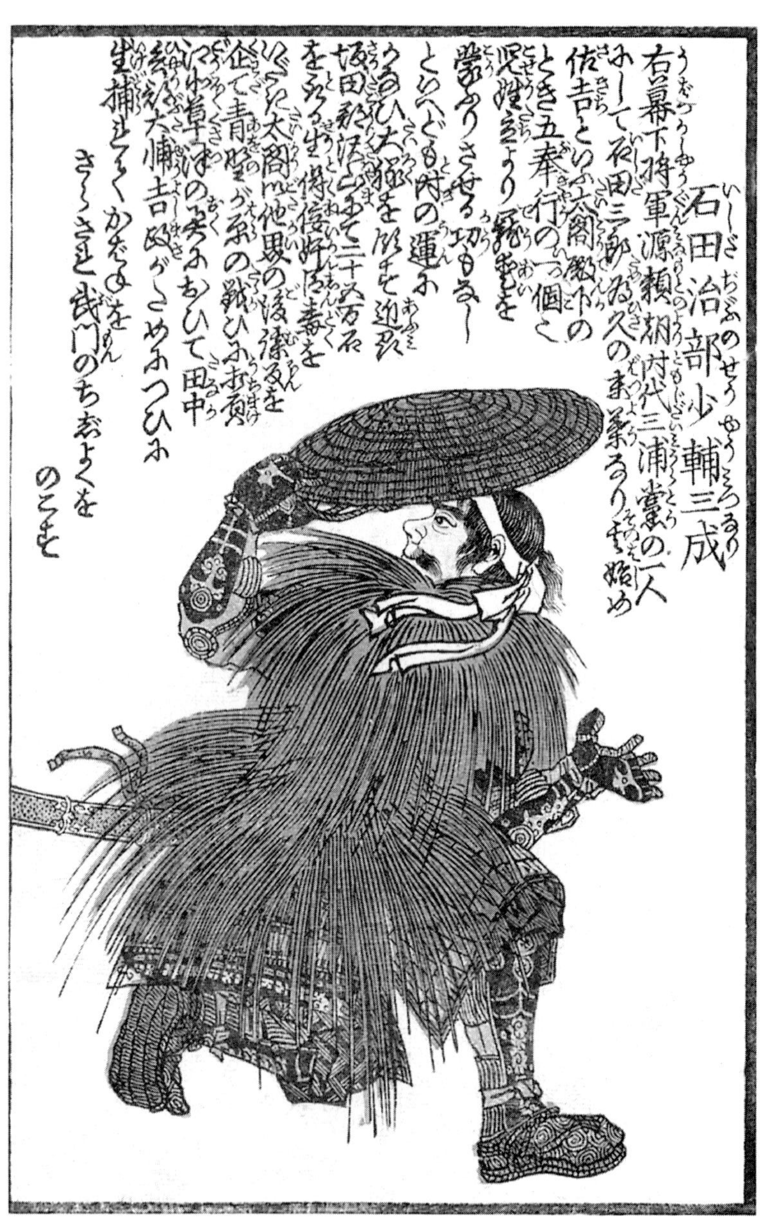

Plate 102

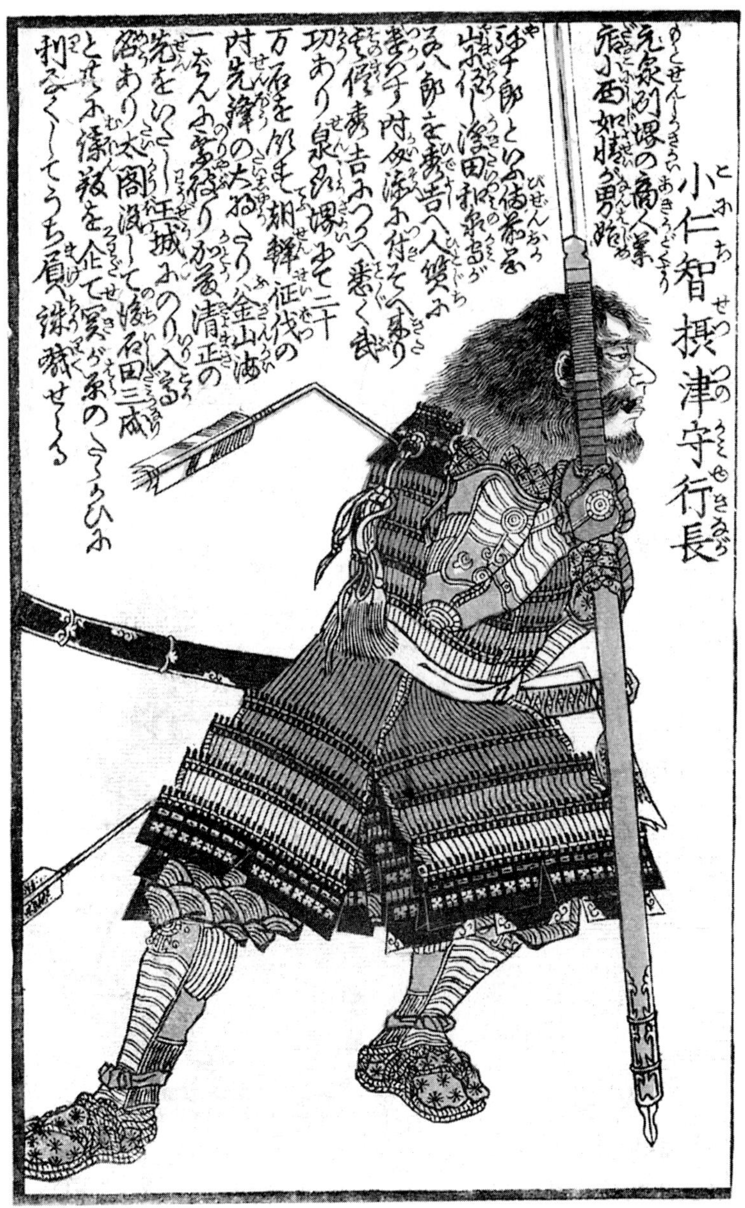

PLATE 103

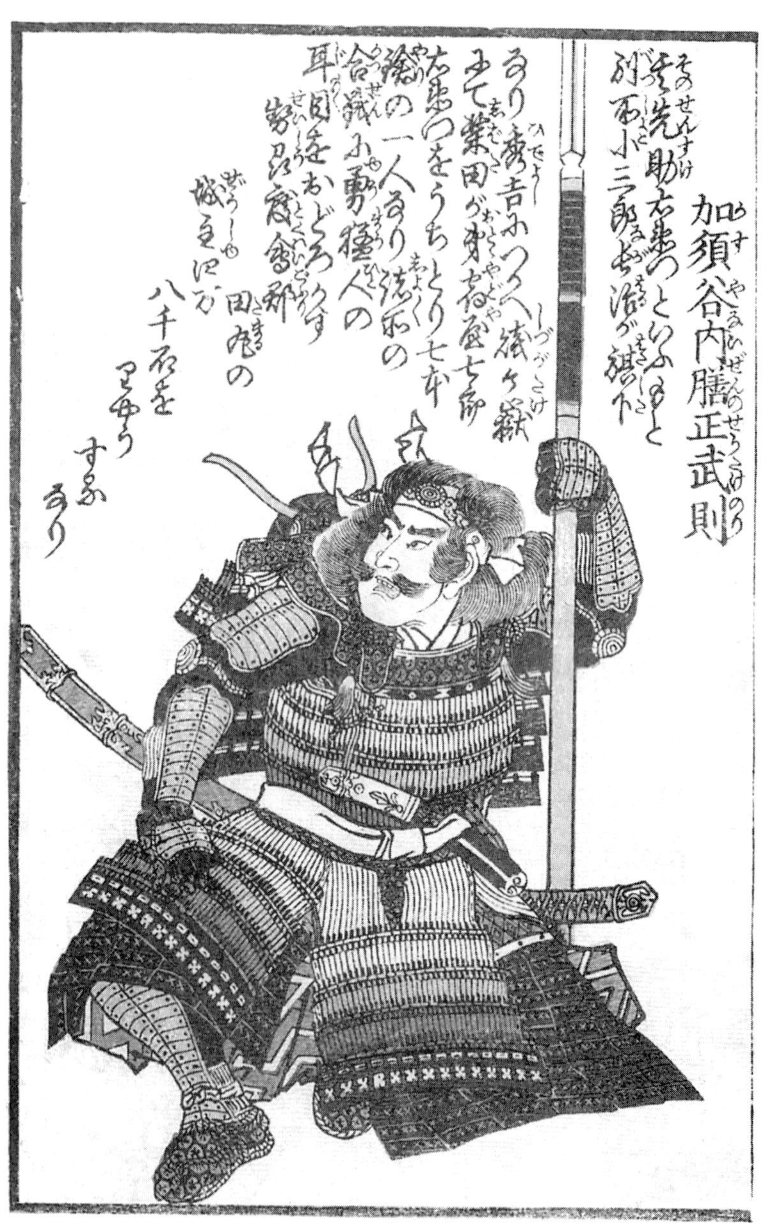

PLATE 104

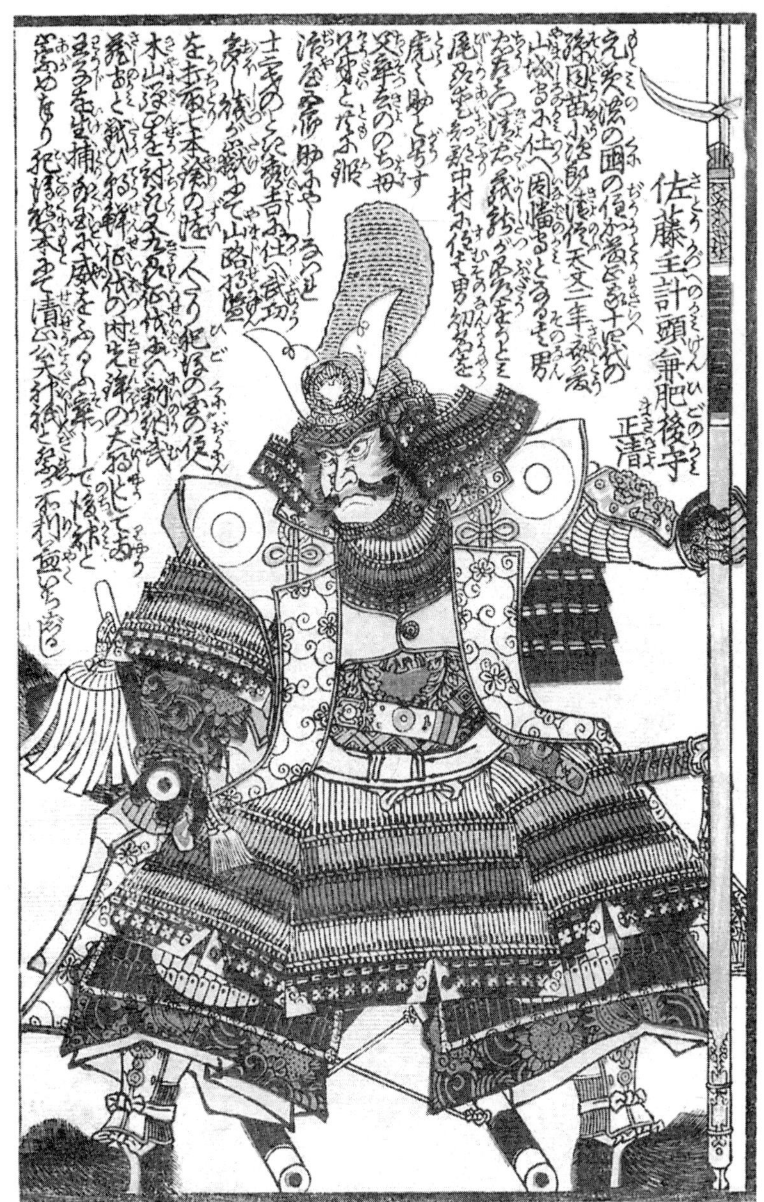

PLATE 105

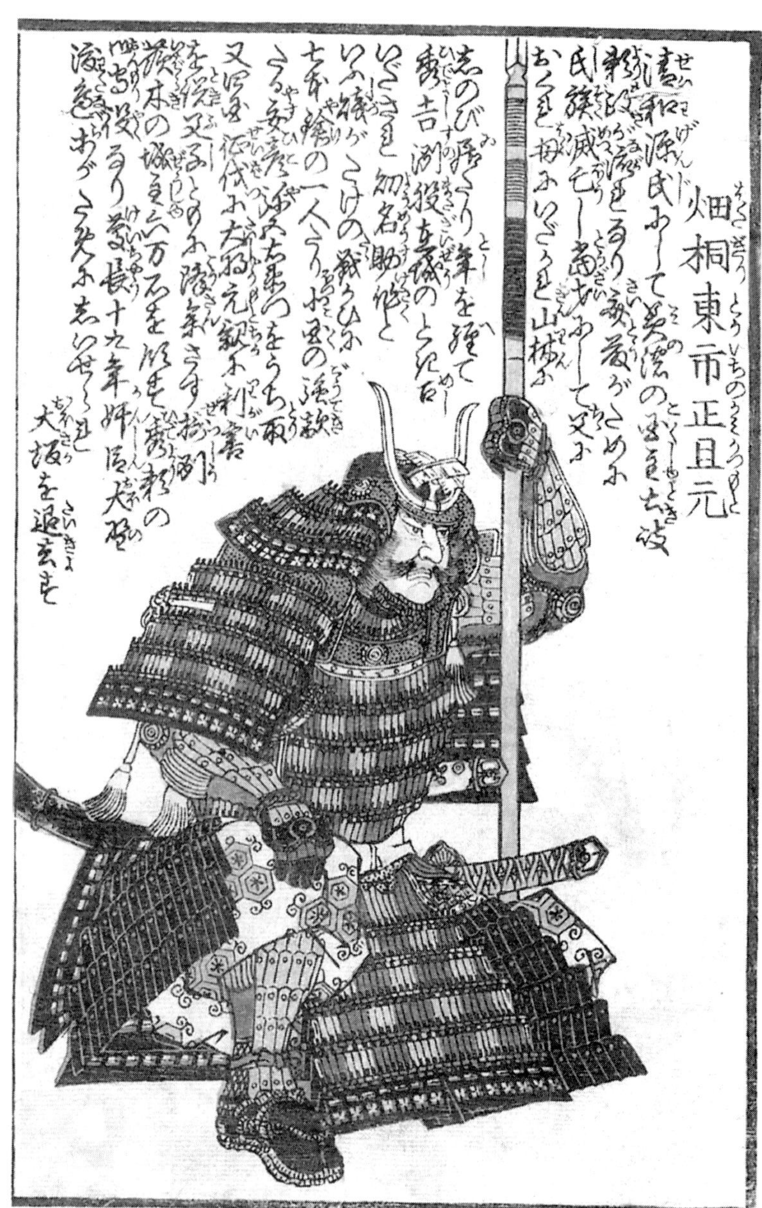

PLATE 106

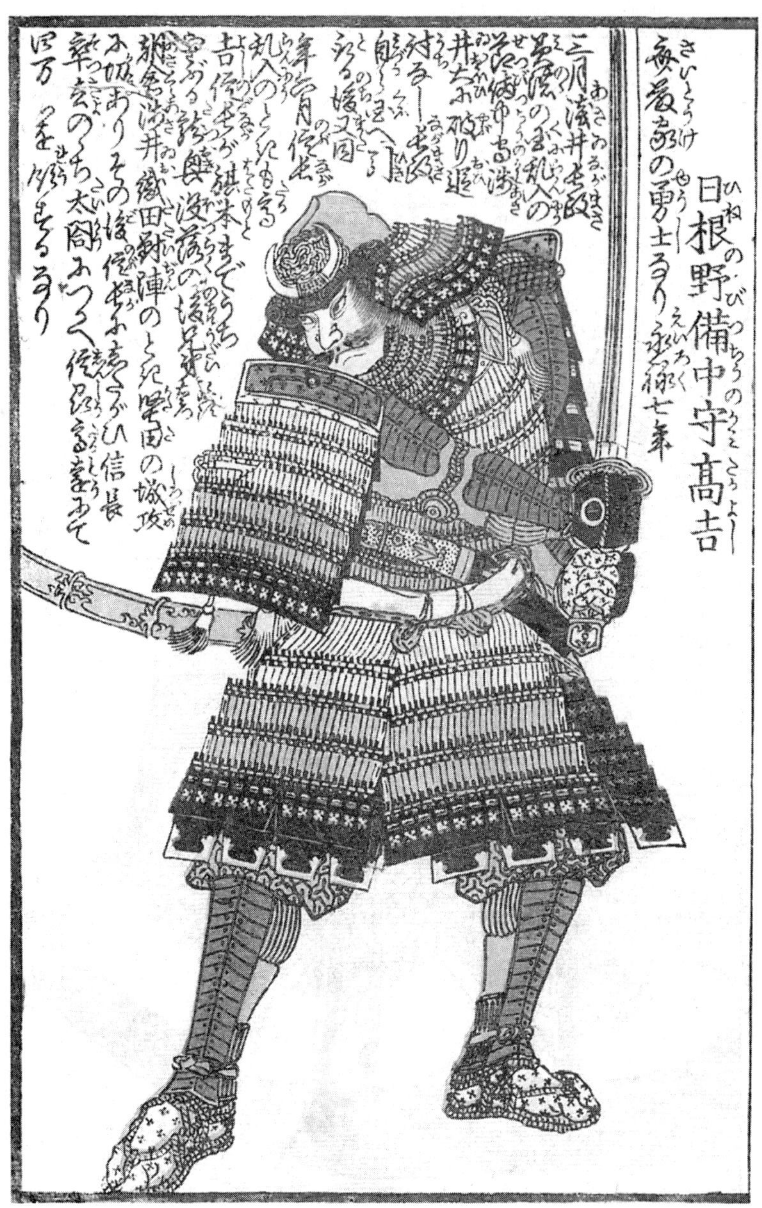

PLATE 107

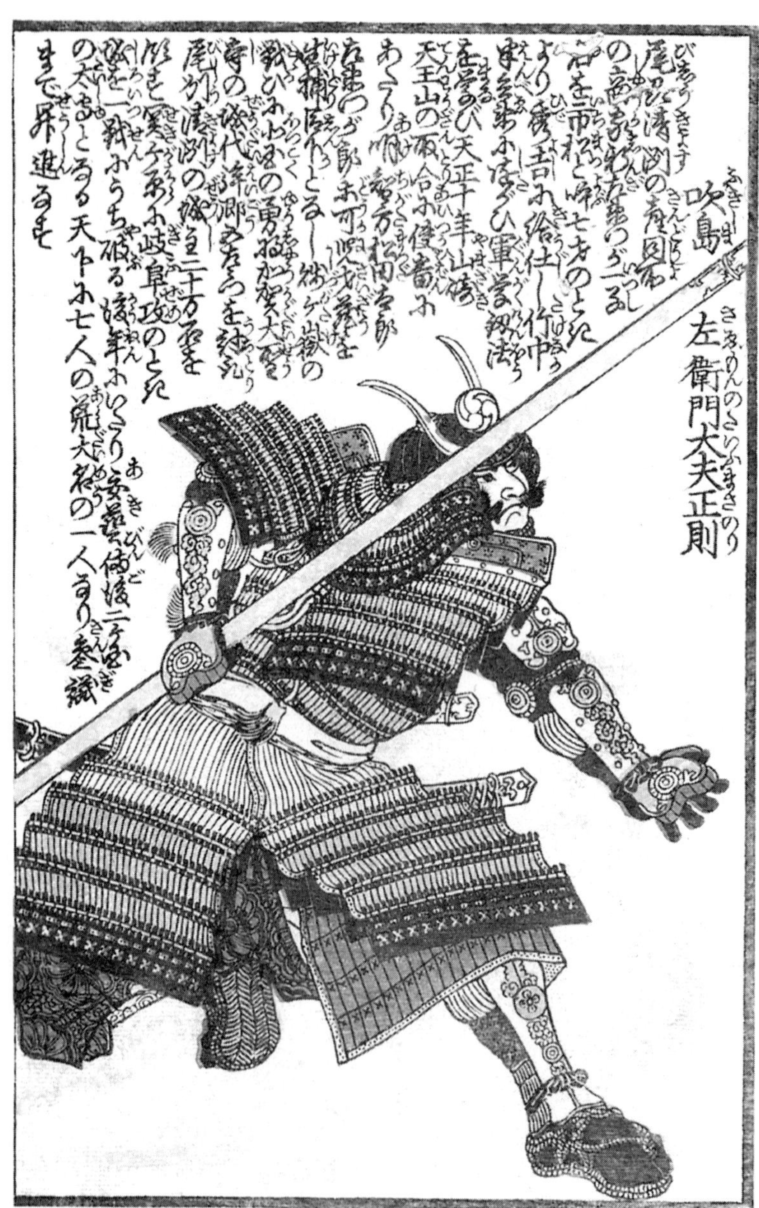

PLATE 108

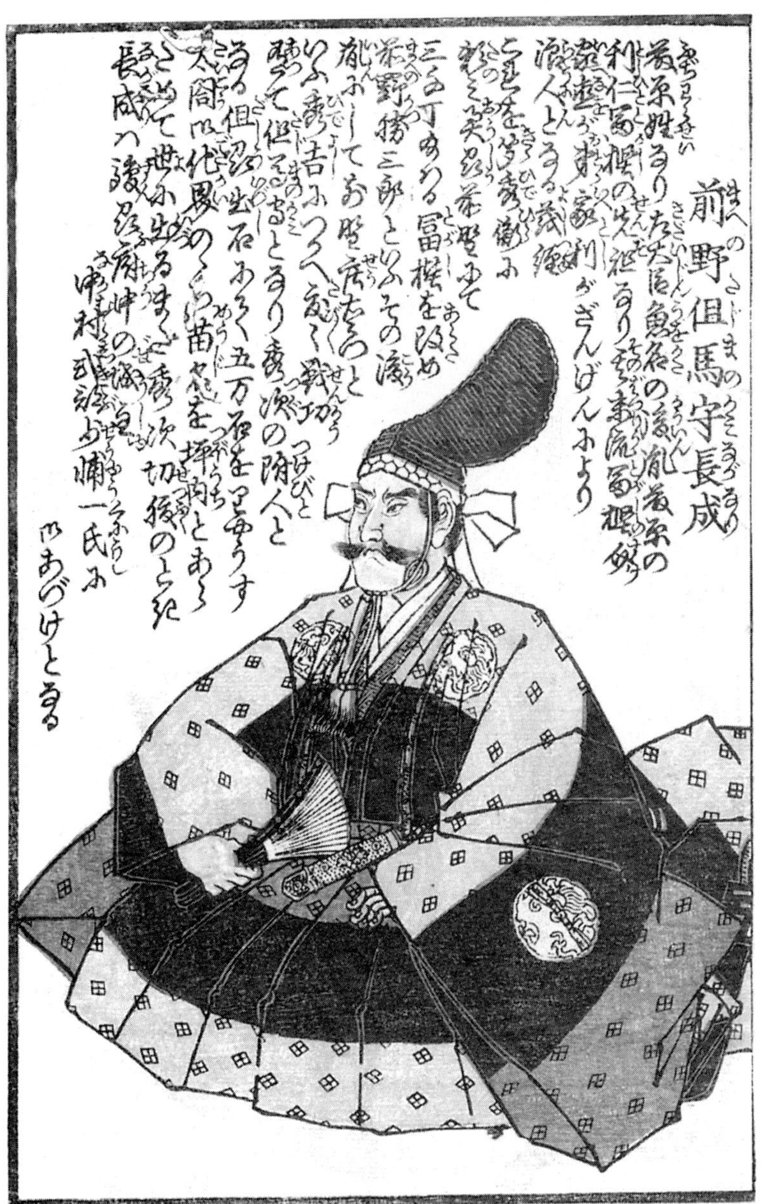

PLATE 109

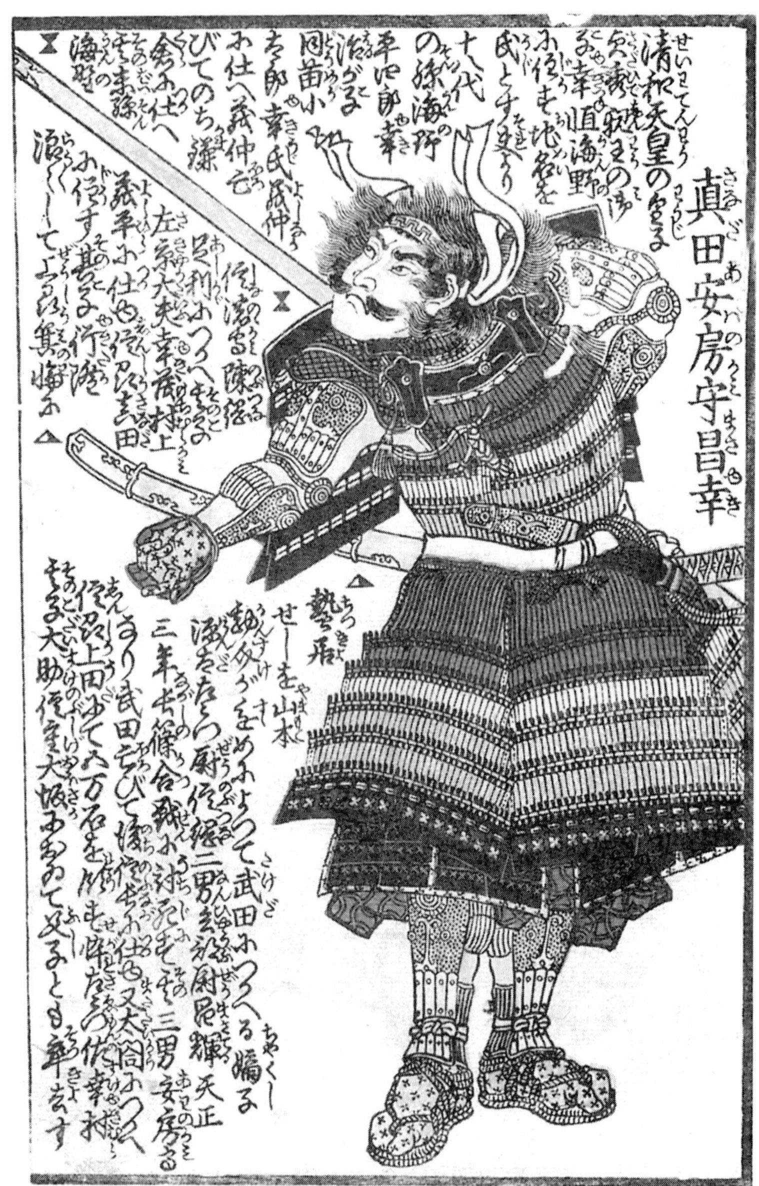

PLATE 110

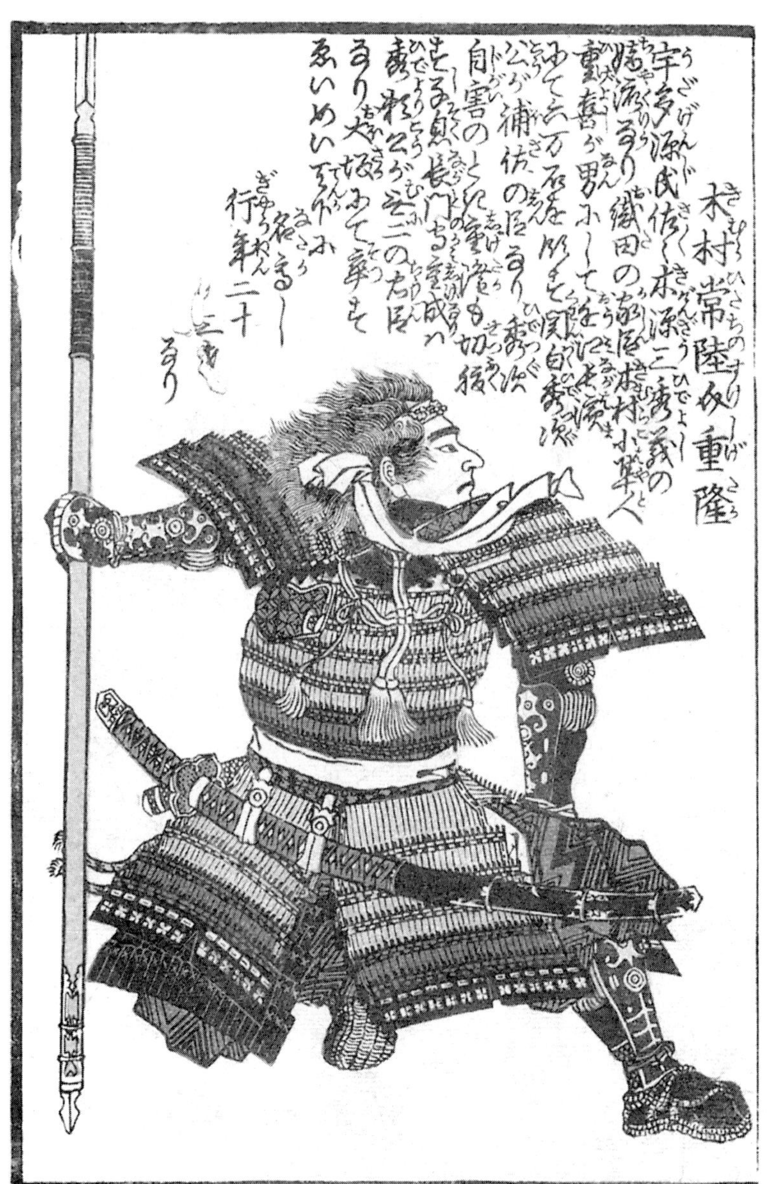

PLATE 111

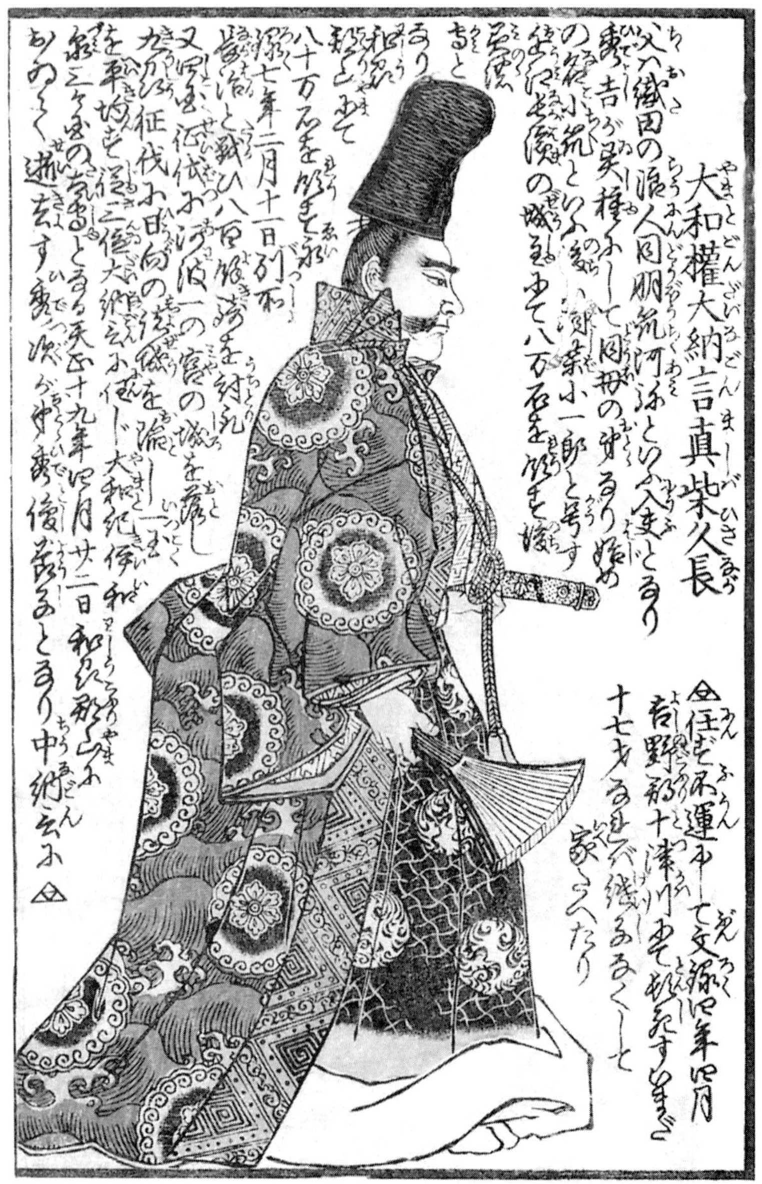

PLATE 112

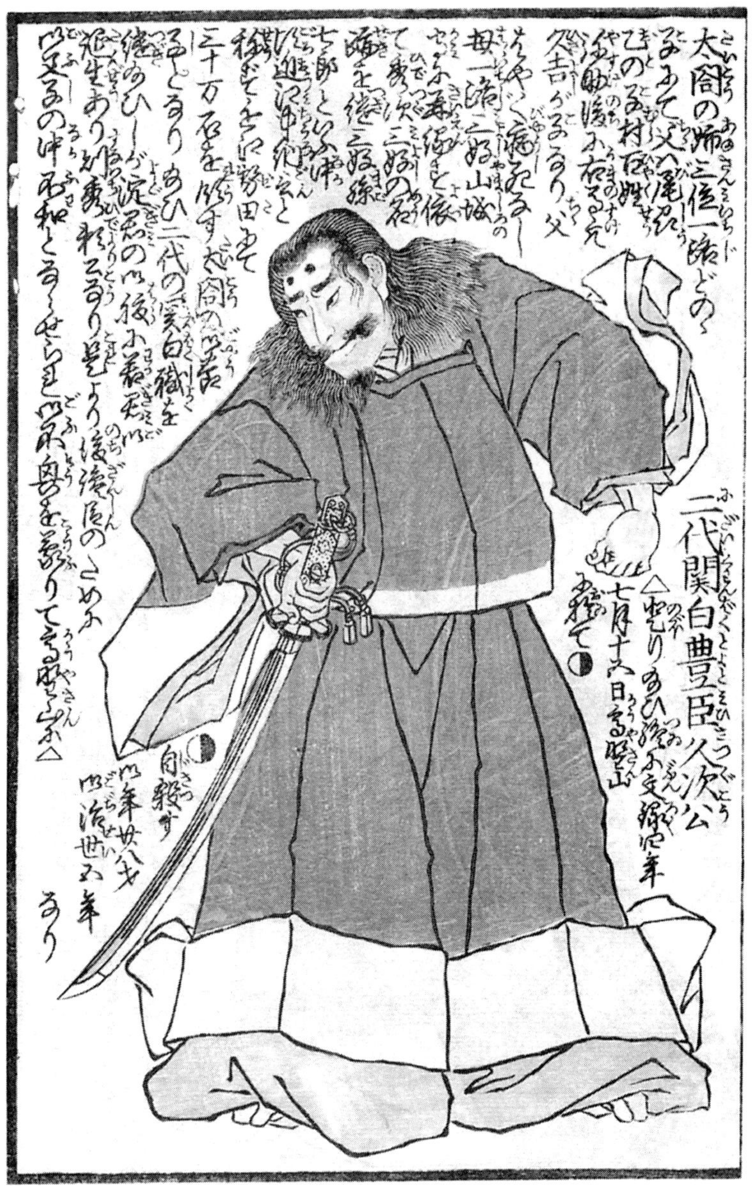

Plate 113

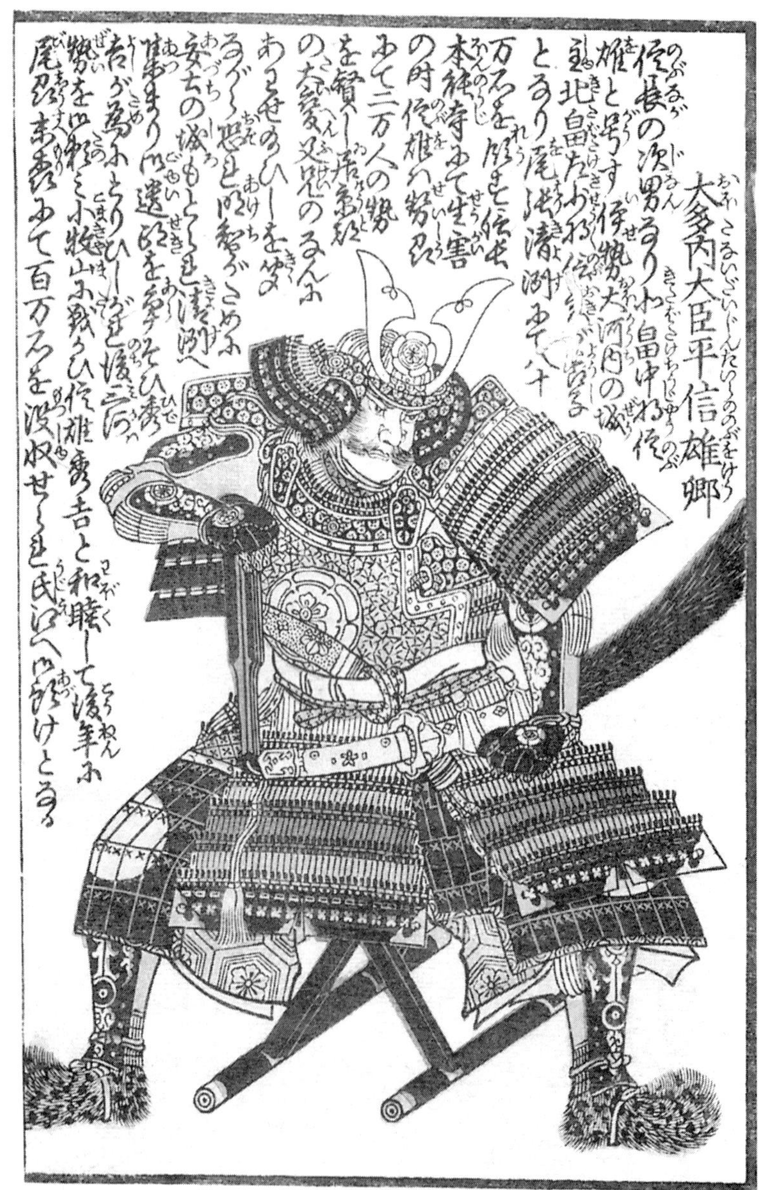

PLATE 114

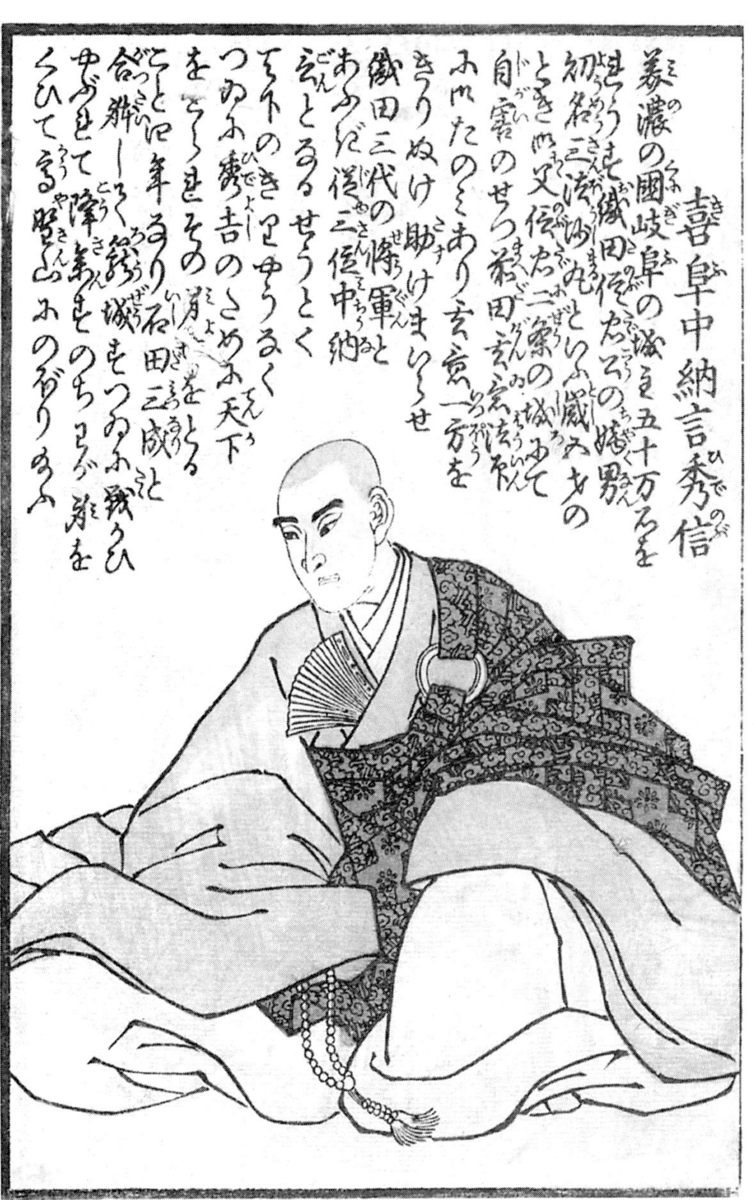

PLATE 115

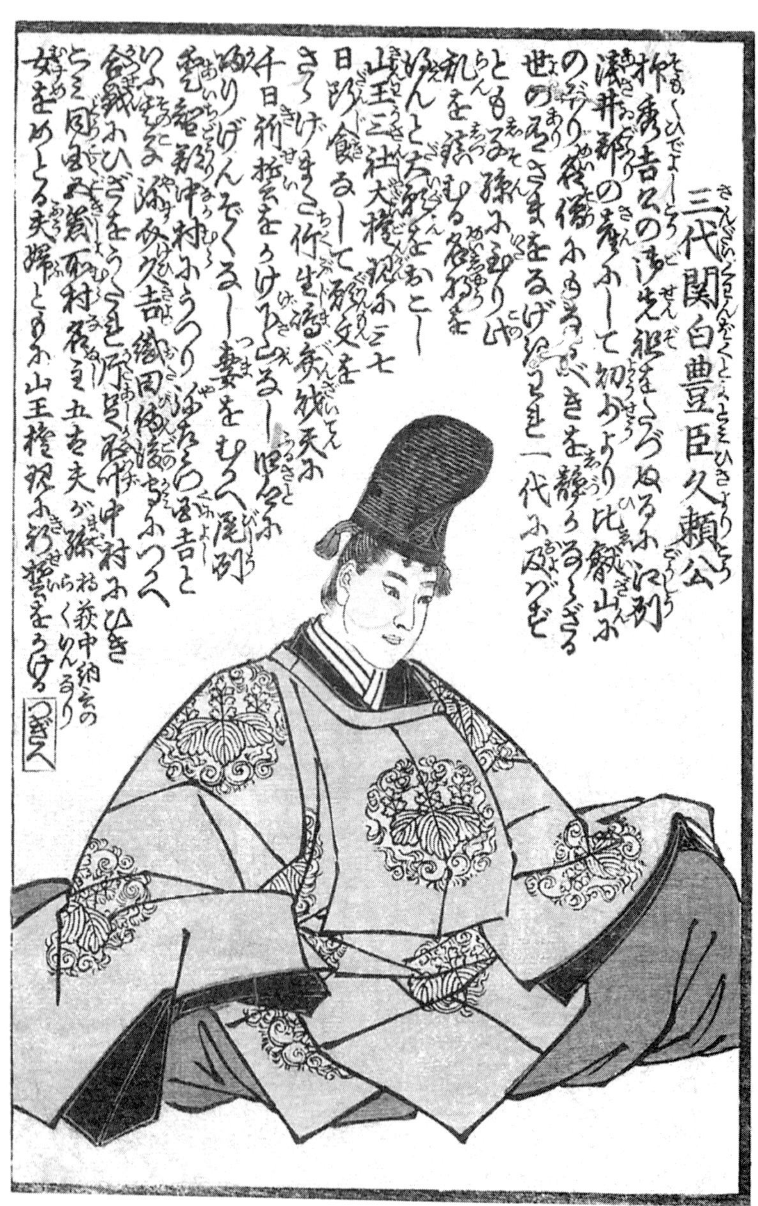

PLATE 116

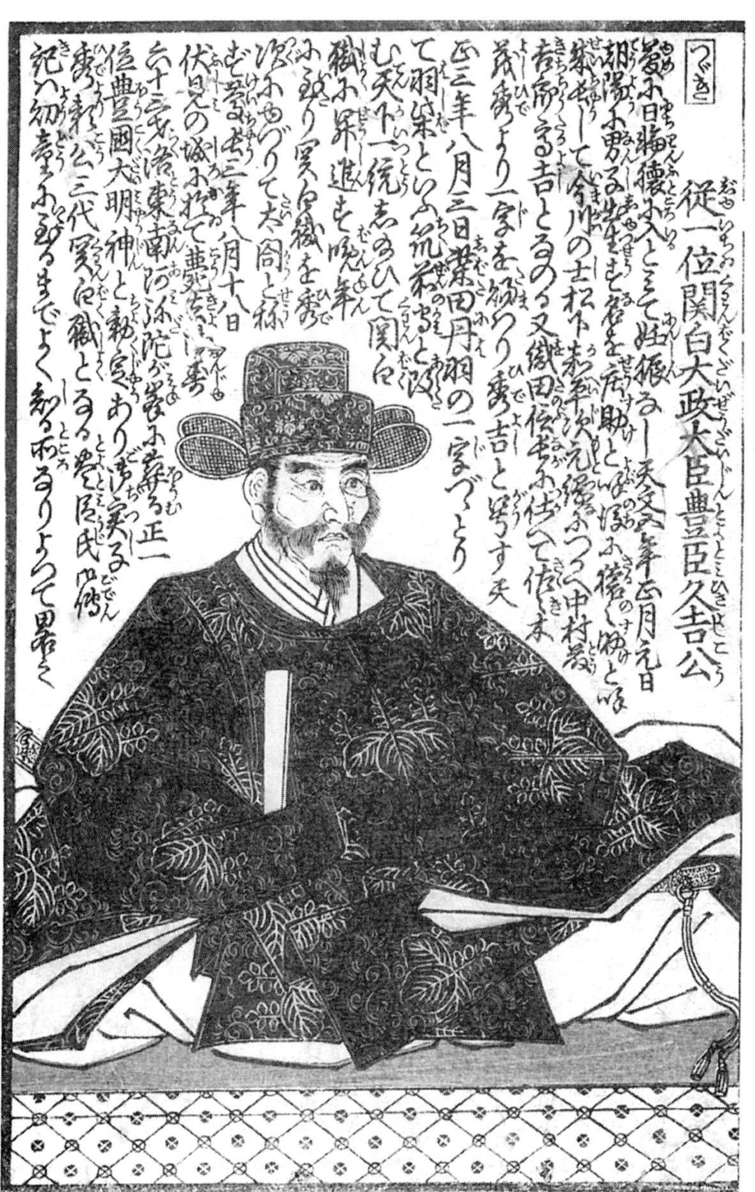
つゞき
従一位関白太政大臣豊臣久吉公